A Vision for the World Economy

Integrating National Economies: Promise and Pitfalls

Robert Z. Lawrence (Harvard University), Albert Bressand (Promethee), and
Takatoshi Ito (Hitotsubashi University)
A VISION FOR THE WORLD ECONOMY: OPENNESS, DIVERSITY, AND COHESION

Barry Bosworth (Brookings Institution) and Gur Ofer (Hebrew University)
Reforming Planned Economies in an Integrating World Economy

Ralph C. Bryant (Brookings Institution)
International Coordination of National Stabilization Policies

Susan M. Collins (Brookings Institution/Georgetown University)
Distributive Issues: A Constraint on Global Integration

Richard N. Cooper (Harvard University)
Environment and Resource Policies for the World Economy

Ronald G. Ehrenberg (Cornell University)
Labor Markets and Integrating National Economies

Barry Eichengreen (University of California, Berkeley)
International Monetary Arrangements for the 21st Century

Mitsuhiro Fukao (Bank of Japan)
**Financial Integration, Corporate Governance, and the Performance of
Multinational Companies**

Stephan Haggard (University of California, San Diego)
Developing Nations and the Politics of Global Integration

Richard J. Herring (University of Pennsylvania) and Robert E. Litan
(Department of Justice/Brookings Institution)
Financial Regulation in the Global Economy

Miles Kahler (University of California, San Diego)
International Institutions and the Political Economy of Integration

Anne O. Krueger (Stanford University)
Trade Policies and Developing Nations

Robert Z. Lawrence (Harvard University)
Regionalism, Multilateralism, and Deeper Integration

Sylvia Ostry (University of Toronto) and Richard R. Nelson (Columbia University)
Techno-Nationalism and Techno-Globalism: Conflict and Cooperation

Robert L. Paarlberg (Wellesley College/Harvard University)
**Leadership Abroad Begins at Home: U.S. Foreign Economic Policy after
the Cold War**

Peter Rutland (Wesleyan University)
Russia, Eurasia, and the Global Economy

F. M. Scherer (Harvard University)
Competition Policies for an Integrated World Economy

Susan L. Shirk (University of California, San Diego)
**How China Opened Its Door: The Political Success of the PRC's Foreign
Trade and Investment Reforms**

Alan O. Sykes (University of Chicago)
Product Standards for Internationally Integrated Goods Markets

Akihiko Tanaka (Institute of Oriental Culture, University of Tokyo)
The Politics of Deeper Integration: National Attitudes and Policies in Japan

Vito Tanzi (International Monetary Fund)
Taxation in an Integrating World

William Wallace (St. Antony's College, Oxford University)
Regional Integration: The West European Experience

Robert Z. Lawrence
Albert Bressand
Takatoshi Ito

A Vision for the World Economy

Openness, Diversity, and Cohesion

THE BROOKINGS INSTITUTION
Washington, D.C.

Copyright © 1996
THE BROOKINGS INSTITUTION
1775 Massachusetts Avenue, N. W., Washington, D.C. 20036

Library of Congress Cataloging-in-Publication data:

Lawrence, Robert Z., 1949–
A vision for the world economy: openness, diversity, and cohesion
p. cm. — (Integrating national economies)
Includes bibliographical references and index.
ISBN 0-8157-5184-2 (cl: alk. paper) — ISBN 0-8157-5183-4 (pa: alk. paper)
1. International economic integration. 2. Commercial policy.
3. Competition, International. I. Bressand, Albert. II. Ito, Takatoshi,
1950– . III. Title. IV. Series.
HF1418.5.L39 1996
337.1—dc20 95-21051
CIP

9 8 7 6 5 4 3 2 1

The paper used in this publication meets the minimum requirements of
American National Standard for Information Sciences—Permanence of Paper
for Printed Library Materials, ANSI Z39.48-1984

Typeset in Plantin

Composition by Princeton Editorial Associates
Princeton, New Jersey

Printed by R. R. Donnelley and Sons Co.
Harrisonburg, Virginia

Foreword

A T THE END of the twentieth century a new vision must emerge to guide international policy. Because almost every aspect of domestic policy now has international ramifications, tension between economic integration and the autonomy of the nation-state poses a challenge both to those who are responsible for defining national economic policy and to those seeking to foster multilateral cooperation. The challenge holds both peril and promise. Attempts to press for expanded national autonomy could further complicate needed international cooperation and fragment the global economy. Relying exclusively on competitive pressures to resolve international tensions could undermine efforts to establish sensible multilateral standards and rules. Yet there is also the promise of creating a more substantial international community reflecting such values as openness, diversity, and cohesion while achieving a balance among them.

In this book the authors present proposals to help realize this promise. They review developments that are forcing the world to look beyond reduction of at-the-border trade barriers and explore alternative ways of dealing with these global changes. They propose a new paradigm of international governance suited to a world of deeper integration as new technology, corporate strategies, and international market pressures undermine the traditional separation between the domains of international and domestic policy. The authors offer a blueprint for a world of clubs in which the nation-state remains a fundamental political unit but joins with other nations in pursuing common objectives. Besides multilateral institutions, functional clubs, regional clubs, and a club of clubs may help create the global community most likely to ensure respect and prosperity for all.

This book, the capstone of the Integrating National Economies series, expresses the views of the authors. It also builds on results from the individual studies of the Brookings project on Integrating National Economies, listed in the front of this volume, and perspectives of the participants from many nations at regional conferences held in Mexico City, Tokyo, and Paris in mid-1994 and at meetings of the World Economic Forum at Davos in January-February 1995.

The authors are deeply indebted to Henry Aaron for extensive comments and editorial assistance on the project. They also thank Ralph Bryant and Susan Collins at Brookings, C. Fred Bergsten and members of the Institute for International Economics in Washington, the many participants in the meetings who offered comments, and other participants in the Integrating National Economies project, especially Richard Herring, Anne O. Krueger, Robert Litan, Pietro Nivola, Robert Paarlberg, and F. M. Scherer. Charles Oman and Raymond Vernon also made valuable comments.

At Brookings Theresa Walker and James Schneider edited the manuscript. Laura Amin, David Bearce, and Gerard Trimarco verified it, and Kathleen Elliott Yinug provided administrative assistance. Princeton Editorial Associates prepared the index.

Funding for the project came from the Center for Global Partnership of the Japan Foundation, the Curry Foundation, the Ford Foundation, the Korea Foundation, the Tokyo Club Foundation for Global Studies, the United States-Japan Foundation, and the Alex C. Walker Educational and Charitable Foundation. The authors and Brookings are grateful for their support. Brookings also gratefully acknowledges the assistance of BANAMEX, Electricité de France, Nomura Research Institute, and Promethee in helping to make the Mexico City, Paris, and Tokyo meetings possible and successful.

The views expressed in this book are those of the authors and should not be ascribed to the persons or organizations whose assistance is acknowledged above, to the authors' current or past employers, to organizations with which the authors are or have been affiliated, or to the trustees, officers, or staff members of the Brookings Institution.

MICHAEL H. ARMACOST
President

January 1996
Washington, D.C.

Contents

Chapter 1

The Postwar Paradigm

THIS BOOK and the project Integrating National Economies focus on the tension between two fundamental features of the world at the end of the twentieth century. First, the world is organized politically into nation-states with sovereign governments. Second, growing economic integration among nations is eroding differences among national economies and undermining their autonomy.

Since the end of World War II the predominant goal of international policy has been to achieve free trade. At the same time, however, national sovereignty over domestic policies has been preserved. We refer to this approach as *shallow integration*. By the early 1970s, however, departures from this policy were becoming evident in response to macroeconomic and financial interdependence among nations and concerns about nontariff barriers and the global commons. Nevertheless, pursuit of shallow integration has remained the overriding approach to international governance.

Liberalization and International Governance

In the second half of the twentieth century, achievements in liberalizing trade and investment have been remarkable. In the early 1950s the world was still suffering aftereffects from the inward-looking, beggar-thy-neighbor policies that had helped plunge the world into the Great Depression of the 1930s. The legacy of the 1930s was a fragmented world of impoverished

1

national economies separated by restrictive quotas and high tariffs
and by tight restrictions on currency conversion, capital movement, and direct foreign investment.

Today, border barriers have almost disappeared among developed countries. Import quotas are rare and industrial tariffs are
low. Capital flows freely across the borders of most developed
countries, and many developing countries and foreign investors
are welcome and free to establish and operate businesses on the
same basis as domestic residents. Cross-border mergers and
acquisitions and the globalization of portfolios have also developed rapidly. Extraterritorial (Euro) markets, offshore centers,
and a general trend toward deregulation and financial innovation now give private parties unprecedented freedom in making
international investment decisions.

These policy developments have been reinforced by innovations
in technology and communications. In combination, they have
produced the most rapid half century of economic advance in
world history. In the first half of the period, the United States
enjoyed unprecedented growth, but Europe and Japan grew even
faster, so that their incomes converged rapidly toward U.S. levels.
In the second half of the period, growth in developed nations
slowed, but many developing countries, particularly in East Asia,
grew spectacularly. Other nations, especially in Latin America,
experienced periods of slow growth and inflation, but they appear
back on track after a lost decade. In the late 1980s the ideological
confrontation between East and West evaporated, and former communist countries began the transition to capitalism. At the same
time many developing countries privatized and liberalized. Although many developing countries experience major difficulties,
and most of Africa and much of the Middle East has stagnated,
most developing countries are committed to outwardly oriented,
market-friendly policies, and an increasing number are committed
to democracy.

National policies and international institutions, as well as market forces, have contributed to these developments. In the 1950s
the United States dominated the world economy. It accounted for
almost half of total output and led all other nations in industrial

technology. Geopolitical concerns and economic interests led the United States to promote a multilateral world economic system based on open trade. This approach succeeded spectacularly. Europe and Japan assumed important global roles. The Soviet empire first languished and then collapsed.

European integration paralleled these worldwide trends. After western Europeans failed at creating a European Defense Community in the 1950s, they used economic integration for both economic and political purposes, thereby increasing their prosperity and creating lasting bonds among countries that have often been at war with one another. Although episodes of europessimism have occurred—most recently in the wake of the difficulties in ratifying the Maastricht Treaty—Europe has led trade liberalization on two occasions, first in the 1960s, when it created a common market with a lower common tariff than the previous national tariffs, and again in the 1980s, when member countries embarked on an unprecedented effort of regulatory convergence designed to achieve a single European market.

Throughout the postwar period, international institutions and agreements have nurtured and promoted liberalization. Meetings and treaties after World War II laid out the blueprint for the world economic order. Leaders recognized that open trade and a stable international financial system were the keys to successful reconstruction of the world economy. The Bretton Woods conference, held in 1944, chartered the International Monetary Fund (IMF) and the International Bank for Reconstruction and Development (the World Bank). The Bank was to enhance financial flows to both war-battered and underdeveloped economies. The Fund was to help establish a new monetary system that would prevent the beggar-thy-neighbor, floating exchange rate policies of the 1930s by implementing a system of fixed (but adjustable) exchange rates with parities based on gold or the U.S. dollar. In particular, the Fund would help provide liquidity to member countries to allow them time to adjust their external accounts without changing their exchange rates—a practice permitted only in the face of fundamental disequilibria. The aim was a system that would let countries pursue the domestic goal of full employment and yet discipline exchange rate behavior.

A series of meetings ending in Havana in 1948 set out a charter for the International Trade Organization and the General Agreement on Tariffs and Trade. This charter aimed at achieving free trade and preventing the reemergence of the preferential groupings that had divided the world economy of the 1930s. GATT, in particular, sought to achieve free trade through reciprocal tariff reductions and to ensure that countries would give equal treatment to all contracting partners. The key was most-favored-nation treatment. Although the ITO was not ratified by the U.S. Congress (nor by the governments of many nations) and never came into being, GATT became the centerpiece of the international trading system. Multilateral negotiations under the auspices of GATT began in 1947, and in seven rounds, the most recent of which, the Uruguay Round, was formally signed in April 1994, dramatically lowered tariffs.

In recent years the Fund and the Bank have provided advice and incentives to developing countries that have complemented multilateral liberalization. By and large, the goals set out at the end of World War II to achieve an open world trading and financial system have been achieved.[1]

Stretching the Limits of Shallow Integration

In the 1950s and 1960s, trade negotiations focused heavily on removing barriers at the borders of countries. National governments retained strong control in other domestic policy areas.[2]

---

1. Besides the Bretton Woods institutions, developed countries have cooperated in both the macroeconomic and trade issues at the Group of Seven (G-7) summits and the Organization for Economic Cooperation and Development. Cooperation among developing countries, by contrast, has been centered in the UN Conference on Trade and Development (UNCTAD). International organizations have also flourished for the purposes of achieving cooperation on issues concerning particular sectors. Examples include specialized UN agencies such as the Food and Agriculture Organization, the International Civil Aviation Organization, and the International Maritime Organization. Other examples include entities that address broad issues, such as the International Labor Organization, and the Bank of International Settlements, which is concerned with international banking policy and facilitating international payments.

2. Driven by the need for containment of the Soviet threat, international governance in the West after World War II encompassed extensive military cooperation, particularly in NATO.

GATT sought to achieve free trade and to obtain nondiscriminatory treatment for foreign goods, but it did not try to harmonize or even to constrain domestic economic policies. Similarly, the Fund emphasized fixed exchange rates and sought to avoid national controls on foreign exchange. But it gave nations considerable latitude in implementing domestic macroeconomic policies and did not try to coordinate international macroeconomic policies. When it came to exchange rate changes, the Fund was often informed rather than consulted.

When the barriers at nations' borders were high, governments and citizens could sharply differentiate international policies from domestic policies. International policies dealt with at-the-border barriers—tariffs, quotas, exchange rates. Domestic policies covered everything within a nation's borders—competition and antitrust rules, corporate governance, product standards, worker safety, regulation and supervision of financial institutions, environmental protection, tax codes, monetary and fiscal policies. Nations were sovereign over domestic policies without regard for effects on other nations. But these sharp distinctions gradually eroded, particularly for international finance, trade, and the global commons.

International Finance

Historians still debate why the Bretton Woods monetary system broke down in the early 1970s. According to one commonly held view, the growing mobility of international capital undermined the system's sustainability.[3] Mobile capital makes it hard to maintain domestic autonomy and stable exchange rates at the same time. If market participants come to expect exchange rates to change, domestic authorities will be forced either to use monetary policy to support the currency or yield to speculative pressures and allow the exchange rate to adjust.

Under article VIII of the IMF, members commit themselves to currency convertibility on the current account, but the Fund's charter is conspicuously silent on commitments to enable capital

---

3. Indeed, the original architects envisaged a system with limited capital mobility. See the papers in Bordo and Eichengreen (1993), especially the article by Eichengreen, p. 623.

flows. Capital liberalization has been an integral part of international integration in the postwar period. As a result, capital market pressures have become increasingly apparent. The Bretton Woods monetary system showed strains in the late 1960s, and the fixed parity system broke down in the early 1970s. The pivot of the system, the convertibility of the dollar into gold at $35 an ounce, collapsed in the face of rapid U.S. inflation. Because other countries quoted their exchange rates in terms of the U.S. dollar, the United States had no mechanism for adjusting its exchange rate. When it ran into balance of payments difficulties in 1971, therefore, it pressured countries with trade surpluses to appreciate their currencies. When these measures proved insufficient, the Bretton Woods system broke down. A brief attempt to restore the fixed exchange rate system at new parities, the Smithsonian agreement, failed, and in 1973 floating rates became the norm.

In a system of floating rates, nations may in principle pursue independent policies but must be prepared to accept the effects of exchange rates on their domestic economies. To avoid these effects, some degree of policy coordination is necessary. The extent of such coordination has varied over the past two decades (box 1–1).

Financial Markets

Networks of financial institutions and markets transmit shocks virtually instantaneously worldwide. The authorities responsible for any one part of the network cannot ignore what happens elsewhere. The collapse of the small privately held Herstatt Bank in 1974 and the disruption it caused for other nations in the interbank market brought home to financial regulators the growing interdependence in financial markets, and the need for clearer lines of responsibility among national authorities.[4] Central bankers in the industrial nations established the Standing Committee on Banking Regulations and Supervisory Practices, the Basel Committee. The resulting concordat, signed in 1975, was the first attempt to clarify supervisory responsibilities. As a result, lines of authority and responsibility no longer corresponded neatly to na-

4. Herring and Litan (1995).

Box 1-1. Policy Coordination

The early high-water mark of policy coordination was the Bonn summit in 1978.[a] The United States recovered more rapidly than other countries did from the recession of 1974–75. As a result, the U.S. current account had declined and the dollar had weakened. The United States and such other industrial nations as Germany and Japan feared that additional dollar declines would cause inflation in the United States and contraction abroad. At the Bonn meeting, therefore, the United States persuaded its allies to stimulate their economies in return for an American agreement to deregulate domestic energy prices. While debates continue over the consequences of the agreement—and carrying it out was complicated by the second OPEC oil shock in 1979—the agreement was widely blamed for the acceleration of U.S. inflation, the continuation of deficit-financed government expenditures in Japan, and a loss of fiscal discipline in Germany.

Partly in reaction and partly because of changed circumstances, policy coordination was minimal during the first term of the Reagan administration. U.S. policy was focused on internal matters. A combination of tight money and easy fiscal policy produced a strong dollar and large U.S. trade deficits. The pendulum swung back to policy coordination among the three economies in 1985, however, because of concerns that U.S. policy was not sustainable. On September 22, 1985, monetary authorities from the United States, the United Kingdom, Japan, Germany, and France met at the Plaza Hotel in New York City, agreed that the dollar was overvalued, and launched a program of monetary coordination to reduce its value. In the following months the United States lowered its domestic interest rates and Japan and Germany raised theirs. The Louvre accord, concluded in February 1987, initiated a period with target zones for exchange rates. The five Plaza accord nations plus Canada and later Italy agreed to keep their currencies within an unannounced band. Exchange rate fluctuations between 1987 and 1989 were reasonably mild. In subsequent years, however, this system has not been much in evidence.

Coordination has sometimes resulted in policies that are inconsistent with domestic goals. Some countries, such as Japan, now look back on the coordination exercise with mixed feelings. Indeed, support for exchange rate stability and the need for macroeconomic policy coordination have fluctuated in the past three to four decades. Nonetheless, the underlying trend toward increased integration has been uninterrupted. The need to deal with external disturbances remains an ever-present problem for macroeconomic stabilization.

Efforts to bring about greater exchange rate stability in Europe paralleled these global developments. The desire to create a zone of monetary stability in Europe led to the founding of the European Monetary System in March 1979, in which major European currencies floated jointly against

---

Box 1-1. (*continued*)

the U.S. dollar. The EMS devised a specific mechanism through daily cooperation among central banks, unlimited short-term credits, and joint decisionmaking called the exchange rate mechanism (ERM) to keep bilateral rates within bands. Members in the system proved relatively successful in keeping their exchange rates stable, and the realignments that took place in the first half of the 1980s followed the agreed rules. They were joint decisions regarding the overall parity grid, rather than national devaluation or revaluation. The Maastricht Treaty, signed in 1991, set forth even more ambitious plans. It aimed at a single currency for the European Union by the end of this century. Among the first steps taken to complete the internal market was the decision in June 1988 to require the lifting of all capital controls by July 1990. Capital mobility complicated the task of the EMS. Problems in maintaining the European Monetary System in 1992–93 somewhat damaged prospects for achieving a fixed exchange system gradually and made it more likely that the single currency will be implemented by a "hard core" of half a dozen countries rather than all European Union members.

a. Putnam and Henning (1989).

---

tional jurisdictions. Host countries were given primary responsibility for providing emergency liquidity of foreign banking affiliates. Home countries were responsible for supervising their solvency.[5] Subsequent failures, such as the collapse of Banco Ambrosiano and the Bank of Credit and Commerce International (BCCI), have forced revisions and additions to these rules. Concerns about international risks to the banking system also led to the accord on capital adequacy announced by the Basel Committee in July 1988 and later incorporated into the national regulatory systems of member countries.[6]

Trade

An increase in concern over the international ramifications of domestic policies is also evident in the area of trade. Early GATT

---

5. Secrecy laws have actually made this difficult to apply. Herring and Litan (1995).
6. Herring and Litan (1995).

negotiating rounds focused on lowering tariff barriers.[7] But as these barriers fell, it became increasingly apparent that other domestic policies could affect trade flows by creating nontariff barriers. Such policies included technical barriers to trade, methods of customs valuation, import licensing, subsidies to domestic companies, government procurement from domestic companies, and antidumping and countervailing duties. Launched in 1973 and completed in November 1979, therefore, the Tokyo Round added codes to GATT to cover these issues. In several cases the codes limited domestic autonomy, but the constraints were modest, and GATT's ability to settle disputes remained weak.

Governments have been increasingly drawn into dealing internationally with behind-the-border issues. The most striking example in the 1980s occurred in Europe. The European Community of the early 1980s became aware that its much celebrated Common Market was not so common after all. Nontariff barriers, national regulations, and private practices with a strong national bias had replaced many of the official barriers that had been removed in July 1968. The business community helped reveal the unsatisfactory and incomplete nature of liberalization measures. In particular, the European Business Roundtable, a nonprofit coalition of the leading European high-technology companies, commissioned analyses and published reports assessing the cost that differences in domestic regulations and standards were imposing on European companies. A white paper, written by European Commissioner Lord Cockfield in 1984, built upon the findings and recommendations of the European Business Roundtable. In turn, this report and the 297 specific measures it included became the cornerstone of the program to create a unified internal market by 1992, as agreed on by the European heads of state and government at the 1985 Luxembourg summit and as ratified by their national parliaments in the form of the Single European Act.

At first sight this "Europe 1992" program could be seen as a pragmatic collection of additional measures to open national markets. But the measures could also be seen as a bold strategic

---

7. Efforts were made at the Kennedy Round to deal with nontariff issues, but these did not result in any agreements. Low (1993, p. 173).

initiative aimed at implementing the three freedoms: freedom of movement for goods, capital, and people. These freedoms go well beyond the shallow integration paradigm. In particular, movements of people include movements of labor. Already nine of the fifteen members of the European Union have agreed to suppress all border controls in the framework of the Schengen Agreement. Similarly, the freedom of movement for services entails not only the right to establish but also to deliver services across borders and the right to do so under the regulations of the country of origin rather than under the regulations of the country of destination. Obviously, such a freedom would have been difficult to grant in the absence of some standardization of at least the most important regulatory criteria, a condition that many of the 297 measures in the Europe 1992 program were precisely designed to achieve.

The freedom granted to European companies as part of the internal market for services goes beyond these elements of regulatory standardization. Nonstandardized national rules can be dealt with under the principle of mutual recognition. As embodied in the 1979 ruling by the European Court of Justice known as *Cassis de Dijon,* this principle of mutual recognition implies that member nations accept as legitimate regulations by other countries that depart from theirs. A common approach to competition law and stringent restraints on state aids are among other features of the European internal market that clearly go beyond shallow integration.

The Uruguay Round, which lasted from 1986 to 1994, continued to lower tariffs but also took noteworthy steps toward broadening and deepening the scope of GATT. For the first time, new areas of services were introduced and agriculture came under international rules similar to those for industrial trade. The Uruguay Round also introduced new rules for trade-related intellectual property rights and investment measures. It revised and extended the Tokyo Round codes and established the World Trade Organization (WTO) with a mechanism for settling disputes that, unlike the earlier version, could not be thwarted by the country accused of failing to live up to its obligations. In several areas, particularly intellectual property rights, the Uruguay Round agreement represents a further diminution of domestic autonomy. In addition, it has increased international interest in negotiated standards for competition policy, foreign investment, and labor and environmental protection standards—all subjects on which the Organization for Economic Cooperation and Development (OECD) has already conducted in-depth reviews and discussions.

Global Commons

Limits to Growth, a report issued by the Club of Rome in 1972, contained serious analytical flaws, but it encouraged academics, governments, and the public to look at the world as an integrated system and to become increasingly concerned about the global commons.[8] Countries negotiated agreements to limit acid rain and other forms of pollution, to supervise exploration of the deep seabed, to reduce use of chemicals that deplete the ozone layer, to control toxic waste trade, and to govern exploitation of Antarctica. Institutional innovations, such as the creation of the United Nations Environment Program in 1972 and the holding of global conferences on population (Bucharest, 1974), desertification (Nairobi, 1977), and alternative and renewable energy sources (Nairobi, 1981), did not succeed in establishing genuine international regimes, but the conferences did create a much higher awareness of the resource constraints that nations should deal with together.

At the urging of UNEP, countries began to discuss a more precise agenda associated with the preservation of regional seas. A result was the 1976 agreement on a Mediterranean action plan by sixteen countries, twelve of which also agreed to control specific types of pollution, to regulate dumping, and to cooperate in the event of an oil spill or other environmental emergency. In 1980 a "sources protocol" was added to establish a detailed list of substances to be controlled. These agreements are not yet fully effective but, in Tony Brenton's words, they are "nevertheless striking testimony to the persuasive power of the scientific consensus, coupled with the growth of the habit of environmental cooperation among the Mediterranean nations," and "there is also good evi-

8. Meadows and others (1972).

dence that the process has given a boost to the evolution of domestic environmental policy, and the influence of domestic environmental ministries."[9]

The third UN Conference on the Law of the Sea (UNCLOS III), which lasted from 1973 to 1982, addressed matters of marine law, from fish conservation to environmental protection. Extravagant hopes for exploration of the mineral wealth on the ocean beds led UNCLOS to declare such reserves "the common heritage of mankind." But the agreements took effect only in 1994 when the required sixty countries had ratified the treaty, and the likelihood of cooperation is much in doubt.

The early 1980s were a time of reduced international activity regarding the global commons. But private initiatives and nongovernmental organizations preserved the momentum in other forums. The International Union for the Conservation of Nature and Natural Resources (IUCN) quietly helped many countries establish national conservation plans along the lines of the World Conservation Strategy that it had adopted in 1980 with UNEP support. The organization's most important initiative during the 1980s was the formation of the Brundtland Commission. In 1987 the commission put forward the concept of sustainable development, namely, development that "meets the needs of the present without compromising the ability of future generations to meet their own needs," thereby striking a productive compromise between protection and growth.[10] The 1984 Bhopal accident in India, the Chernobyl nuclear accident in 1986, and the Cherno-Basel fire in a Swiss factory that polluted the whole Rhine River in 1986 made clear that borders do not stop threats to the global commons. The late 1980s, then, saw a new, massive rise in the importance attached to environmental issues by public opinion in most developed countries and many developing countries.

Developing countries that had only reluctantly joined the international environmental debate were shocked when Nigeria in 1988 found children playing among 8,000 drums of toxic waste of Italian origin at its port of Koko. The Organization of African

---

9. Brenton (1994, pp. 99–100).
10. World Commission on Environment and Development (1987, p. 43).

Unity at its May 1988 Addis Ababa meeting was instrumental in generating worldwide soul searching about the $3 billion annual trade in toxic waste from northern to southern countries. In March 1989 the Basel Convention on the Transboundary Movements of Hazardous Waste established an international regime of "informed consent" under which importing countries had to be properly notified before toxic waste was shipped to them. The European Community strengthened internal constraints and agreed to limits on shipments of toxic wastes to African, Caribbean, and Pacific countries under the framework of the Lomé IV Convention.

Another important example of binding agreements over the global commons are those associated with Antarctica, a continent administered through regular meetings among the thirty-eight self-proclaimed Antarctic Treaty States. A convention was signed in June 1988 to impose strict environmental controls on any mineral prospecting and extraction on the continent. At a June 1991 Madrid meeting twenty-four countries, including the United States, agreed to replace the convention with a fifty-year moratorium on mining minerals in Antarctica.

Binding decisions have also been taken in other frameworks. The 1987 Montreal Protocol set ambitious targets to reduce production of CFCs, gases considered harmful to the ozone layer, by 50 percent by the year 2000. Governments in developed countries agreed to help developing countries financially and technologically and to set up a new international institutional structure in which a permanent secretariat arranges for information and data exchange, international financial assistance, and regular meetings of experts and government officials. Clearly, such initiatives go well beyond the type of cooperation embodied in shallow integration.

The June 1992 Earth Summit in Rio de Janeiro adopted two important conventions on climatic change and biodiversity. These nonbinding conventions commit countries to report on national policies to deal with climate change and to preserve biological diversity. The "climate change" convention creates important pressure on national policies, as illustrated by the decision of the Clinton administration that the United States would also try to reduce emissions of carbon dioxide to 1990 levels by 2000.

The Cairo conference on population in 1994 triggered a worldwide debate about demographic trends and the values with which the various nations are approaching these common issues. Although the world is far from agreement on many of these values, nations understand that these issues are matters of more than domestic concern and are prepared to discuss common approaches openly.

A New Threshold

Viewed separately, the measures that have been taken on financial regulations, regulatory matters, and environmental protection can be seen simply as incremental expressions of international concerns over issues once regarded as domestic. Viewed together, they reflect a new threshold in global economic relations and in the relations between governments and their citizens. This threshold in turn results from fundamental developments in technology, corporate strategies, and the integration of global markets.

Technology

The relaxation of government barriers to trade and investment has had dramatic effects because it has been reinforced by a new wave of technological change. Technology has reduced the effective economic distances among nations by lowering the costs of moving goods, services, money, people, and information.

Such innovations have increased knowledge of potentially profitable international exchanges and of economic opportunities abroad. And this process is continuing. Airplanes now on the drawing boards will carry 500 to 1,000 passengers on nonstop flights of more than fifteen hours, making it possible for large numbers of people to circle the world with a single stopover. The International Telecommunications Union conference in Torremolinos in 1992 set aside radio frequencies for the development of global communication networks able to operate between any two points on the planet without use of installed ground networks. A dozen international consortia are already competing to realize this potential. Technical capacities—

global positioning systems, pictures of the earth's surface with a one-meter resolution, and private virtually global networks—that were reserved to a few military forces only four years ago are now available to the public at attractive prices.

This technological revolution is not confined to Manhattan, the Ginza, and the Right Bank in Paris. China, which had only about 4 million telephones in the early 1980s, now has about 20 million and according to estimates will have 100 million by the turn of the decade. Today more than 20 million global Internet users share knowledge, insights, and emotions as easily as residents of a small town did a generation ago.

With increased travel and improved communications, not only the issues but also the actors have been internationalized. Citizens, firms, and associations are linked internationally in relationships that sometimes bypass and sometimes pressure their national governments. Organizations and associations pursuing particular agendas cooperate internationally, strategically forming alliances to pressure national and international governments to promote their interests. For instance, labor unions in Mexico bring pressure to bear on their government through forging relationships with U.S. unions that can in turn lobby the U.S. government. Nongovernmental organizations have become increasingly important substitutes and complements for official aid and assistance.

The revolution in communications is best captured by the revolution in news broadcasting as the cable news network CNN links the world, instantaneously bringing viewers into contact with crises in other parts of the world, sometimes at the same time as, or even before, such news reaches their governments. Public opinion responding to such news becomes an important source of pressure on government action.

Changes in technology that are shrinking the economic distances among nations would have progressively integrated the world economy even in the absence of reductions in border barriers. Reductions in barriers would have encouraged interdependence even without the technological innovations. Together, however, these evolutionary changes have reinforced each other and strikingly transformed the world economy.

Corporate Strategies

Lower trade and investment barriers combined with technological advances in communications and transportation have stimulated firms to expand trade and investment in two ways. National differences in factor endowments and technological capabilities have led to increased interindustry trade and investment, particularly between developed and developing countries. The most dynamic developing countries have promoted manufactured exports. Those with the best export prospects, because of low wages, diligent workers, and political stability, have been especially successful in attracting foreign direct investment.

Among developed countries, income levels have converged because these nations enjoy similar technological capabilities, have similar amounts of capital per worker and workers with similar education, and use similar managerial practices. As countries become more similar, intraindustry trade and investment increases. Companies with a market niche at home try to exploit similar demand and production opportunities abroad. This trade is especially concentrated in industries with highly differentiated and technologically advanced products or in which product variety and economies of scale are important.

To compete effectively in sophisticated, high-technology products often requires a significant domestic presence for marketing, sales, and service. Foreign trade and investment have therefore become complementary. The ability to follow market trends, respond to customer needs, and acquire innovative smaller firms in all major markets has become essential for success. The international diffusion of innovations has also become increasingly rapid. The diminished time it takes for competitors to respond to new innovations makes access to large global markets essential for spreading the fixed costs of innovation.

Direct foreign investment has grown even more rapidly in services than in goods production. The essence of many services is that they are produced and consumed in the same place. Deregulation of sectors, such as telecommunications, transportation, utilities, and finance, is driving services investment. Communication and information technology now allows multinational companies to function as global companies with a speed, efficiency, and depth that was impossible ten years ago. Companies such as ABB, Nissan, and DEC run not just flows of components but tightly integrated production and distribution processes across borders. The economies of speed made possible by today's global networks have already taken the real world far beyond the internationalization that the architects of the postwar order could have imagined in their wildest dreams.

Global Markets

With their expansion and integration, international capital markets place increasing pressures on governments (box 1–2). Under the Bretton Woods system, a 5 percent shift in currency values was a major international event. International markets achieve such changes now in a matter of days and sometimes minutes. Markets pass judgment on government actions continuously, judgments that governments ignore at their peril.

The first effect of the operation of global markets is therefore increased volatility. By their reactions and their natural tendency

---

Box 1-2. Scapegoating

It is tempting to blame globalization for all manner of domestic failures. Since the first oil shock, for example, overall economic performance in OECD countries has been poor. Average real wage growth has been slow in the United States, and the wages of unskilled U.S. workers have actually declined. Unemployment has increased in Europe. Growth has recently slumped in Japan. Because this poor domestic performance has coincided with the increased globalization of these economies, many blame foreign trade and investment for their problems. Somehow, all three regions are disturbed at their "declining international competitiveness."

In fact, such U.S. problems as slow overall income growth and increasing inequality are predominantly driven by slow productivity growth in services, changes in technology, and other domestic factors. Europe's unemployment problems reflect the inability of domestic markets to adjust to change. And the restoration of Japanese growth depends heavily on domestic deregulation and reform.

to overshoot, markets can make specific types of national policies very costly to maintain. In 1994, for instance, Italy raised its interest rates. Markets saw in this step a loss of control by the Italian government over macroeconomic fundamentals rather than an orderly policy process. The resulting plunge in the value of the lira forced the Italian government into a new round of stronger policy measures.

Global markets can even force governments into steps that may put them at odds with preferences expressed by voters. In the summer of 1993, for example, the pervasive market judgment appeared to be that French unemployment rates were so high as to call for a much more rapid reduction in short-term interest rates than was possible in the framework of the European Monetary System. Yet the French and German governments were adamant that their national economic interests would be better served by sticking to monetary systems convergence, even at the cost of high unemployment in France in the short term. The only way that these perspectives could coexist was by widening the bands within which European currencies could fluctuate and accepting de facto devaluation of the franc. One year later, the French and German central banks could feel vindicated because European currencies had returned to the previous European Monetary System grid, an event market participants felt would be politically and economically unsustainable. Whoever was right on that matter, the episode showed that critical decisions on national economic policies were made not simply within the national institutional and political setting but within a broader arena in which market participants from all over the world had a say. This experience reveals that the views of national governments and the views of free markets can surely clash.

Pressures and Frictions

As national differences narrow and the intensity of competition increases, business decisions on where to locate become more sensitive to differences in domestic policies and practices. Paradoxically, the more similar countries are, the more significant their

remaining differences become in determining trade and investment flows. As the barriers of protection are lowered, the diver-
gences among remaining domestic policies and practices have
become apparent.

Mobility and the Internationalization of Policy

As factors of production become mobile, regulations and taxes
that raise local production costs become increasingly expensive. In
a closed national economy, producers can either reduce production or bear the cost of the regulation or tax. In an open economy,
they can shift production abroad. As these locations become closer
substitutes, the ease of relocation increases, forcing governments
increasingly to take account of other countries' regulations in
making their own choices. Multinational companies that plan to
produce in one country and sell in others seek secure and internationally compatible operating rules, intellectual property rights,
and technical standards and regulations. Those seeking to attract
and keep them, therefore, inevitably feel pressures to comply. The
resulting pressures on national policy are especially important
because national governments have assumed increasing responsibility for the living standards and quality of life of their citizens.
The mismatch between the obligations assumed by governments
and their ability to satisfy them while acting autonomously is
growing.

The increased importance of direct foreign investment for corporate strategies leads to a greater emphasis on market access for
companies as well as products. The importance of access in turn
leads to frictions resulting from differing systems of corporate
governance and rules of operation. Even where border barriers are
removed, for example, the weak enforcement of antitrust policies
can lead to collusion that limits new market entry. The focus has
thus shifted from trade policies to competition policies. Similarly,
increased competition in telecommunications, finance, transportation, and media inevitably brings attention to differences in
domestic regulations. When all nations owned or regulated government telecommunications systems, their differences were relatively
inconsequential for one another. But once some nations privatize,

deregulate, and allow some foreign access, the issue of asymmetrical access becomes more relevant.[11]

For example, all major industrial nations now have a significant presence in high-technology industries. These nations also have extensive national innovation systems designed to foster high-technology activities. Yet the systems all treat foreign and domestic companies differently. As competitive pressures build up, attention focuses on the differences. Foreign companies trying to compete with U.S. companies complain that federal defense programs give U.S. companies an unfair advantage. Foreign companies trying to compete with European companies allege that industrial policies give European companies an edge. And non-Japanese companies allege that Japanese markets are closed.

Moreover, concerns about fairness are not confined to business. Labor complains of *social dumping*, competition from foreign products produced in countries with particularly lenient labor and social standards. Environmentalists complain of *ecodumping*, competition from companies in countries with lax environmental protection standards. The groups fear that such foreign competition will force the erosion of domestic labor or environmental standards. In all of these cases, genuine concerns are intermingled with an opportunistic use of these arguments for protectionist reasons.

The End of the Cold War

For much of the postwar period, fully fledged shallow integration brought together like-minded democratic countries who shared most fundamental values or who were willing to downplay their disagreements because of the precarious balance of international power. Meanwhile the communist countries struggled to maintain their own integration regime around the Council for

---

11. One telling example was the realization by Europeans that they had provided third countries with new levels of access to the European banking and financial services markets through the creation of the single banking passport created by the second banking directive. If such opening was part of a GATT package, Europe would have been able to ask for something in return. Indeed, the United States used conditional most-favored-nation status as its yardstick for the conduct of trade liberalizations in the Uruguay Round in telecommunications.

Mutual Economic Assistance, and many important third world players, such as Mexico and India, either stayed out of GATT or tried to protect themselves from too much integration by erecting high tariff barriers and following policies aimed at self-sufficiency. The end of the cold war and the breakup of the Soviet Union mean that economic relations are no longer taking place under military threat. Soviet hegemony is no longer suppressing nationalism in central and eastern Europe. Today, almost every country seeks to become part of the international capitalist community. The result has been to increase the importance of economic sources of friction at the same time as geopolitical mechanisms for containing conflicts have been weakened. In the past, when developed countries sought to join the international capitalist community, they were embraced and their internal political practices largely ignored. But today, with the end of the cold war, these issues have become increasingly important. On the one hand, the result has been a welcome spread of democracy. On the other, departures from democratic practices are the subject of conflict.

Political Failure

Political failure is alleged to occur when a country disregards universal or nonnational values. Belief that political failure can occur rests on a rejection of untrammeled political sovereignty for nation-states. Those who hold this view would constrain the exercise of individual nations' sovereignties through international negotiations or, if necessary, stronger intervention.

These concerns have been apparent in international intervention in domestic conflicts in countries such as Haiti where democracy has been undermined, in U.S. efforts to link China's most-favored-nation status to its adherence to human rights, in the agreement within the European Union over the Social Charter, in the side agreements of the North American Free Trade Agreement (NAFTA) relating to labor standards and the environment, and in the proposals by the United States to include competition policy, labor standards, and environmental protection issues on the post-Uruguay Round agenda.

In many parts of the developed world, poor domestic economic performance and revelations of corruption among government officials have led to a great disenchantment with government at all levels. These have not created conditions that are favorable for international governance, and, international institutions are particularly vulnerable to these trends. Indeed, even when not to blame, they make an easy target for those seeking a scapegoat. Thus, while the need for international governance has increased, the capacity to implement such governance has been greatly reduced.

In sum, pressures from divergent national practices, international spillovers, and the erosion of the global commons are leading to direct challenges to national sovereignty. These challenges have sparked heated political controversy and have placed new demands on global governance.

Cross-border economic integration and national political sovereignty have increasingly come into conflict. The effective domains of economic markets have come to coincide less and less well with national governmental jurisdictions. National governments and international negotiations must increasingly deal with deeper, behind-the-border integration.

Chapter 2

The Impact of
Contending Forces

WE HAVE described the pressures for deeper integration. In this chapter we consider three responses to these pressures and then construct scenarios that explore their implications.

Responses

The controversy over the pressures described has been considerable. Political forces are mobilizing on three fronts. Some believe that extensive cooperative efforts are unnecessary, some that increased international cooperation is essential, and some that it is necessary to reverse liberalization to restore the autonomy of the nation-state. Currently, we can see that particular political forces have aligned themselves in these positions.

Sustain Shallow Integration

Many observers doubt that new international cooperative efforts are needed or feasible. They would prefer to concentrate on reinforcing agreements to keep border barriers low, perhaps out of concern about preserving national diversity, perhaps out of faith that market forces alone will achieve the best results. In the European context, for example, the United Kingdom has been a powerful proponent of maximizing the scope for competition between national policies. Britain has resisted the idea that members of the European Union should adopt such common guidelines in social policy as rules to facilitate negotiations between unions and employers. At the same time, Britain has resisted the ECU as a single European currency that would replace national European currencies, preferring a system in which the ECU would coexist with national currencies.

This view is also common in many nations in Pacific Asia. These economies have enjoyed spectacular economic success under a GATT-based regime. That they view initiatives for deeper integration with some suspicion is not surprising. GATT, with its emphasis on shallow integration in general and on special and differential treatment for developing countries in particular, provides scope for developing countries to follow whatever policies they choose. Those that wish to apply liberal policies are free to do so. Those that wish to protect their industries can easily justify more interventionist actions under the agreement's special provisions. Moreover, the only labor standard in GATT relates to forced labor, and on environmental policies GATT emphasizes domestic sovereignty (as the GATT ruling in favor of Mexico in the tuna case indicated). By contrast, most deeper integration initiatives rest on the assumption of reciprocal obligations. Developing countries and other nations with unusual domestic institutions see this as particularly threatening. Developing nations also object that developed nations are seeking to hold them to standards that the developed countries themselves never achieved when they were poor.

GATT has not only extended its benefits on an unconditional, most-favored-nation basis, but it has done so in an inclusive multilateral setting. Nations in Asia and Africa view with suspicion initiatives such as Europe 1992 and NAFTA, particularly because the nations have not been invited to join these regional agreements. Moreover, the absence of formal regional arrangements within Asia has not prevented successful integration in the world economy and growing intraregional trade.

Proponents of this view prefer to rely on private rather than government initiatives. Diminished autonomy in the presence of market pressures could simply be allowed to persist without explicit international cooperation to deal with them. States in the

United States adopt their own tax systems and set policies for assistance to poor single people without any formal cooperation or limitation. Market pressures operate to force a degree of de facto cooperation. If one state taxes corporations too heavily, it knows some businesses will move elsewhere. (The debates about fiscal federalism in the United States and other nations resemble the emerging international debates about the deeper integration of national economies.) Differences in national regulations, standards, policies, institutions, and even social and cultural preferences create economic incentives for a kind of arbitrage that erodes or eliminates the differences. Such pressures involve not only the conventional arbitrage that exploits price differentials (buying at one point in geographical space or time and selling at another) but also changes in the location of production facilities and in the residence of factors of production. Analysts such as Kenichi Ohmae make the optimistic assumption that such forces of arbitrage can be strong enough to reconcile diversity and openness without further international cooperation.[1]

A Level Playing Field

Rather than rely on free competition to force convergence, nations may harmonize policies and structures to make them more consistent. Strong countries will be tempted to use economic power or political power to achieve results most favorable to them. The policies of both the United States and the European Union have become increasingly concerned with promoting certain forms of deeper integration. Significant changes in the relationship between the United States and the world economy have had dramatic effects on U.S. policy. Perhaps most important, given the primary role of the United States in advocating freer trade, is that in many industries American companies have lost market dominance. This result was inevitable as companies in other nations acquired and competed with the same technology. International trade and investment have become increasingly important for the U.S. economy. Between 1970 and 1980, for example, the share of

---

1. Ohmae (1993)

trade in GNP doubled. In the 1980s the United States experienced a massive influx of direct foreign investment.

As they came under increasing pressures in the early 1980s, American companies began to call for a level playing field. They argued that the U.S. government protected its domestic companies less vigilantly than foreign governments did theirs. Increasingly, therefore, the United States called for international limits on policies formerly thought of as purely domestic in nature and for governance mechanisms to enforce such limits. The growing importance of trade in the United States, combined with the powerful role given by the U.S. Constitution to Congress to engage in trade policy, has increased the politicization of trade policy. The United States is seeking increased access for U.S. companies and products not just by seeking lower border barriers but also by creating hospitable and open foreign domestic economic policies.

As a quid pro quo for entry into the U.S. market, the United States is frequently raising such noneconomic issues as foreign rules regarding the environment, human rights, and labor standards. The United States is also trying to achieve these objectives by using a multitrack approach, relying on unilateral, bilateral, and regional initiatives as well as GATT.

During the 1980s the U.S. government has used its powers under section 301 of the Trade Act of 1988 to target foreign practices not covered under GATT that the United States deems unreasonable. These practices include foreign failure to respect intellectual property or to provide access to telecommunications.

The Structural Impediments Initiative (SII) between Japan and the United States covered U.S. concerns with such ostensibly internal policies as Japan's law against large retail stores, antitrust policies, infrastructure spending, the behavior of its corporate groups, and antitrust policy. It also treated Japanese concerns with U.S. budgetary, credit card, and education and training policies. The European approach has been more concentrated regionally but also more intensive. The EU agenda has always had a strong political motivation.[2] In addition the Europe 1992 initiative re-

2. Wallace (1994).

sulted in part from a deeply rooted perception that merely removing internal tariffs and quotas had failed to give Europe the international competitive benefits that would result from a genuinely integrated single market. In its arrangements with the nations of the former European Free Trade Agreement to form the European Economic Area, the European Community took further steps to extend the scope of many of its rules and laws. The Maastricht Treaty deepened the agenda in ways that presaged economic and political union.

Private companies also seek deeper integration. Companies that plan to produce components in one country and sell in others benefit from common rules and credible governance. Similarly, labor and environmental groups seek common rules and governance to deal with global market pressures. Without such rules, they fear a race to the bottom in setting standards.

Restore National Autonomy

Finally, although not necessarily related to global economic forces, nationalist and ethnic conflicts are rampant worldwide. In many instances groups seek to dissociate themselves not only from international but also national governmental pressures. It is striking that the new era of globalization has coincided with growing pressures for increased local autonomy in such nations as Canada, Spain, and Italy. Various U.S. interests fiercely resisted both NAFTA and the Uruguay Round on the grounds that they compromise U.S. national sovereignty.

Another response to the interactions between domestic and international pressures is to reassert local autonomy. The sense that remote and foreign decisionmakers are becoming increasingly powerful in determining local conditions provokes considerable opposition from those who disagree with the policies being promoted. They therefore seek increased national autonomy. Not surprisingly, economic globalization goes hand in hand with a reaffirmation of individual, cultural, and ethnic identities. Minorities can effectively resist economic measures in the general economic interest of a given country by arguing that the measures threaten those identities. How else can one explain the so-called cultural quotas that require television programming to contain at least 40 percent European content or France's decision to ask all radio stations to devote at least 50 percent of program time to French language songs? Our point is not to take sides but simply to note that identities and values as well as economic reasoning influence the international debate.

In short, value conflicts could possibly stand in the way of what economists would call a first-best world. These values are often embedded in multiple layers of regulations, norms, habits, and self-fulfilling expectations that leave little opportunity for impartial reassessment. Differences in corporate governance imply that similar objectives can be pursued through very different routes in different systems, with major risks of misunderstanding and conflicts.[3] Americans, for instance, dismiss foreign criticism of the importance of lawyers in the United States. Foreigners do not understand why Americans think hostile takeovers are a good way to punish management for poor business performance. Other nations have developed what they consider leaner, speedier, or simply less conflictual ways to reach collective decisions on permissible corporate or individual behavior. Countries will therefore disagree on the proper type of relations between stockholders and managers and the appropriate type of governance.

We have described three responses, each demanding a different global governance paradigm. This suggests three quite different scenarios, each exemplifying one of these paradigms. Actual responses will no doubt embody elements of all three and other variants we have not considered. However, in pure form, these "ideal types" help clarify the strengths and weaknesses each approach entails.

Scenario 1: The Invisible Hand

Market forces could spontaneously produce global convergence in economic policies, gradually rendering national political and cultural considerations irrelevant. In such a process, corporations

3. Fukao (1995).

and investors would force standardization of national policies, regulations, standards, and institutional frameworks by moving investments and production or by other actions that penalize countries that adopt policies regarded as inferior or unfair. If markets operated with textbook precision and speed, these actions would result in an efficient allocation of resources. They would also force governments continually to reassess their policies in light of international benchmarks. These market pressures would establish systemic open competition among technical and regulatory standards of all types.

International governance in such a world would not be necessary because markets rather than governments would determine and enforce all needed regulations. Private companies, associations, and nongovernmental organizations would form international networks and linkages to deal with needs such as arbitration of legal disputes, establishment of international financial networks for banking and trading, and creation of bodies to determine standards and quality. The Group of 30 provides an illustration of this process. The group advocated nine major changes to improve operation of stock exchanges. Several of these changes carried a heavy price tag, including "delivery versus payment" and settlement no more than three days after a trade has taken place. This group had no official mandate and no regulatory authority whatsoever. Nonetheless, stock exchanges worldwide implemented the reforms it advocated. The fiscal policy that the French socialist government chose to follow after 1983 is another example of market-imposed convergence. The lifting of all restrictions on intra-European capital movements in July 1990 led the French to reduce taxes on capital gains, which forced increases in taxes on earned income. These actions were at odds with the socialist program. But the government had to act if it was to prevent individual and corporate investors from taking their money to more friendly fiscal environments.

In the world of the invisible hand, therefore, little international governmental coordination is necessary. Official international institutions remain weak and underdeveloped. Nations maintain open borders for goods, services, capital, and in some cases, labor, and national governments undertake policies independently. In fact this scenario for the most part renders international governmental regulation unnecessary and also causes national governments to atrophy.

Kenichi Ohmae has discussed the political implications of an extreme version of this vision.[4] In his opinion, only a handful of the functions discharged by the nation-state today (defense, foreign affairs, and macroeconomic policy) would be needed if markets operated freely. Decisions on infrastructure, human resources, the environment, and many technical fields would be more efficiently discharged at the subnational level, where detailed knowledge is available and accountability to taxpayers and voters is higher. Thus region-states would gradually succeed the old nation-states as actors in charge of technical decisions and day-to-day management. Analogously, Alice Rivlin has proposed that the U.S. national government leave entirely to the states such functions of government as transportation, housing, labor policy, and many others with which the national government is currently involved.[5]

Under these circumstances, international competition takes place primarily among regional economies, some of which may actually overlap current national boundaries. Ohmae suggests, for example, that cities such as Seattle, Washington, and Vancouver, British Columbia, have more in common with each other than either does with cities outside the Pacific Northwest. In a similar vein, Michael Porter has emphasized that regions rather than nations provide unique competitive advantages.[6] Eventually, therefore, cities or subnational regions may forge closer links with one another than they have with their national governments. Governments in such subnational regional economies will concentrate on providing infrastructure, education, and other local public goods and bolstering the competitiveness of industries vital to the regional economy.

Unable to rely on their national economic authorities for assistance, regions would be forced to create hospitable environments to attract the capital and skilled labor necessary to be internation-

4. Ohmae (1993).
5. Rivlin (1992).
6. Porter (1990).

ally competitive. Because companies, capital, and labor would move freely, pressures to harmonize policies would be powerful.

These pressures raise a serious potential problem. Would nations and regions engage in a race to the bottom as they compete with ever lower taxes and more lenient regulatory standards? With the key exception of redistributive measures, this outcome will not occur if markets function effectively. Regions can remain attractive only by providing services and public goods that match the taxes they pay. Any tax necessary to pay for public services that reflects taxpayer preferences or contributes to productivity will be supportable. For example, in the United States, where local taxes finance public schools, residents of districts with good public schools are generally prepared to pay higher taxes. Similarly, residents are unlikely to vote for governments that turn their societies into havens for pollution or regulation-free zones for multinational corporations. However, a world without border barriers severely limits the capacity of governments to redistribute income. Nations would be able to redistribute income through public spending, taxes, and regulation only to the extent that they could tax immobile factors. For public measures that involve redistribution, therefore, there may well be a race to the bottom.

In terms of pure competitiveness this scenario has much to recommend it. Individuals and companies would move to regions that provide public goods that match their preferences. In addition, governments would be forced to compete in providing services and rules that meet the needs of their citizens. Inefficient and excessively burdensome government bureaucracies would find their tax bases eroded. Similarly, this regime would preserve diversity where it is beneficial and induce convergence to best practices where it was not. In fact, C. M. Tiebout has demonstrated that under certain very restrictive conditions such a regime would provide the optimal supply of local public goods.[7] Moreover, as regions became wealthy and large, they could realize the economies of scale and scope possible by providing public goods that were once achievable only at the national level.

7. Tiebout (1956).

The exceedingly strong assumptions necessary for results to be optimal include the presumed absence of important spillovers among economies.[8] But this condition is bound to be violated when companies, workers, and consumers are all free to move. Indeed, they would all have incentives to consume public services in regions where those services are abundantly supplied but to pay taxes in regions where they are relatively low. Preventing such behavior would be impossible. Companies based in several economies could also develop monopoly powers. Who would be responsible for policing their behavior? Another concern is the neglect of spillovers that are international in scope, such as those generating basic scientific knowledge or preserving the environment. Finally, within the nation-state (given immobile taxable factors) such redistribution is possible. However, in the world of the invisible hand, disparities within and between regions could grow. In this world, aid between nations would be confined to that undertaken by nongovernmental organizations. These organizations do accomplish valuable work, but they cannot satisfy the need for international assistance to the least developed nations. Although it has become popular in some quarters to discount the contributions made by official organizations and institutions in helping these nations, in the world of the invisible hand, those nations unable to compete would surely fare poorly.

The vision of a world governed by market pressures presumes that nations or regions will forbear from geopolitical activities other than those directed at purely economic objectives. The dismantling of borders could indeed spell the end of history outside the narrow realm of market developments. Inevitably, however, some nations would be more powerful than others. Some would try to dominate others. Small nations or regions could well find themselves subject to economic pressures, such as those created by Super 301, or to the political will of the powerful. In short, the invisible international hand would remain out of sight only if all nations were to remain weak or abstain from use of power outside market transactions.

---

8. Stiglitz (1977).

Yet at the same time, the invisible hand scenario rests on the assumption that governments are strong enough to enforce forward-looking domestic adjustment, to redistribute income internally, and to support political modernization. In sum the invisible hand has many attractive elements but can exist only in carefully defined and limited sectors.

Scenario 2: Global Fragmentation

Some political interest groups, such as multinationals, drive the forces of globalization. Other groups are threatened. Even if free trade and investment make nations as a whole better off, they could also increase income inequality and make redistribution more difficult to achieve. Freer trade and investment might lower incomes for workers and capitalists who have enjoyed protected access to domestic markets. Important domestic groups may value such objectives as protecting the environment or preserving the social safety net above open trade and see globalization as a threat to domestic values. During periods of poor domestic economic performance, it is often tempting to try to resolve domestic conflicts by taking steps against outsiders.

Centrifugal Forces

The 1930s provided perhaps the most dramatic example of these isolationist tendencies. In vain efforts to protect themselves from economic recession, nations raised protective barriers in beggar-thy-neighbor policies that stifled both trade and international capital flows and intensified the global depression. Economic slack elicited policies that not only stifled but reversed the movement toward global integration.

For example, the United States could turn away from the crucial leadership role it has taken since World War II and seek to dominate its trading partners through bilateral negotiations. Numerous groups in the United States currently express disenchantment with increased international integration. On the left, some labor and environmental groups portray increased global integration as a threat to labor and environmental standards. On the right, some companies fear unfair international competition, which they characterize as an unlevel playing field. Some nationalists fear that deep integration will undermine U.S. national sovereignty. Such pressures could prevent the extension of NAFTA. Or the United States could establish a hub-and-spoke arrangement, offering preferential access to the U.S. market, particularly for nations in the western hemisphere, in return for preferential treatment for U.S. companies and products. Such an action could divide nations in the Asian Pacific as some took refuge within a U.S.-dominated bloc while others remained aloof or retaliated with protectionist arrangements of their own. It could also result in diverting trade and investment.

Tensions within Europe could hinder the ability of the European Union to function effectively. Opponents of greater union, on the right and the left, could become increasingly powerful in opposition to particular measures adopted by Brussels. Fear of rapid immigration from other European nations and from outside the Union could unleash powerful reactionary forces. Europe could be tempted to give bordering nations preferential access and association while raising barriers and discriminatory measures against goods originating elsewhere or companies headquartered elsewhere.

Tensions could become severe between Japan and other developed nations because of increased rivalry in high-technology competition, continuing perceptions that the Japanese market is closed, or growing dismay at Japanese trade surpluses. The result could be quantitative restrictions by the United States or Europe on Japanese trade and investment. Such sanctions could snowball into discriminatory treatment of other Asian nations whose domestic policies are unilaterally deemed to be incompatible with market-based economic interactions. These measures might provoke increased resentment from Japan and other Asian nations against western nations and increase support for nationalist policies based on discrimination. The risk would be a breakdown of relations among developed nations.

The "Threat" from Developing Economies

Discrimination against developing countries because of their lower wages and weaker labor and environmental protection standards could easily emerge. Groups in both Europe and the United States have blamed trade for high unemployment and slow wage growth. Ross Perot's allusion during the U.S. debate over NAFTA to the "giant sucking sound" of jobs as they moved southward crystallized these fears. Perot and Pat Choate warned against ratifying NAFTA because "once properly trained, Mexican workers' productivity and work quality equals that of anyone, anywhere in the world," which makes it all the more unacceptable that "when benefits are included, the average total compensation in 1992 for Mexican auto workers was $3.33 per hour—one-seventh the $24.21 per hour that was paid their U.S. counterparts."[9] Some U.S. critics of NAFTA feared that the agreement would increase the number of runaway plants, companies that relocate operations to low-wage countries. Similar fears are apparent in the European Union despite its successful addition of low-wage Spain, Portugal, and Greece.

Concerns about unfair international labor competition impinge on wages and labor regulations. Efforts to ensure minimum labor standards throughout the European Union have been an important motivation for forging the single European market. The Hoover Corporation's move from France to Scotland, purportedly because of lower wage costs and weaker labor standards, raised a furor in France. In the debate about freer trade with eastern Europe and Asia, western Europeans have expressed concerns not just about low wages but about social dumping and the resulting downward competitive pressures that trade allegedly places on labor standards. U.S. international trade legislation reflects concerns about workers' rights. Both France and the United States have proposed that the post–Uruguay Round agenda address these rights. The task of maintaining integration between low-wage and high-wage countries will be formidable.

Some developing countries could accept increased labor market standards. Others, however, might conclude that reversing newly implemented, outward-oriented policies costs less than compliance with foreign-imposed labor standards. In addition, resistant

9. Perot and Choate (1993).

governments could blame those standards for one or another of the domestic economic difficulties developing nations inevitably experience. Foreign investors might well shun transitional economies if those economies were denied access to European and U.S. markets. The initial responses of economies in transition and indebted developing countries has been increased immersion in the global economy.[10] Should these policies fail, an inward-looking response could well result. Strong nationalist movements would increase this risk. The following hypothetical chain of events would increase the likelihood of global fragmentation: the World Trade Organization lacks the power to arbitrate trade disputes and the WTO's use of its power provokes powerful nations to quit the organization. If such events materialize, bilateral disputes among industrialized nations would increase and regional groupings would look inward. Even the European Union could split over efforts to establish an integrated currency or closer political union.

Economic-Political Interactions

Political disputes constitute another source of tensions. The debate between China and the United States over human rights illustrates how political values can conflict with desires for economic integration. Repression at Tiananmen Square and repression in Tibet have greatly heightened U.S. sensitivity to abuses of human rights in China. On the Chinese side the move toward a "socialist market economy" exacerbates sensitivities to external interferences even as the importance of access to external markets grows. If China loses access to international institutions and foreign nations raise protectionist barriers against Chinese products, China could again turn inward.[11]

Consequences of Global Fragmentation

In many nations, expectations of growing trade and investment underlie investment flows and asset values, which would be se-

---

10. Bosworth and Ofer (1995); Rutland (forthcoming); Shirk (1994); Haggard (1995).
11. Shirk (1994).

verely reduced in a leaderless and fragmented global system, a serious setback to worldwide economic prospects. Managed trade could replace market-driven trade. Government power rather than consumer preference could determine what is bought and sold.

The stakes in dealing with these conflicts successfully are high. China's booming economy is lifting 1.2 billion people from poverty. Another 866 million people in India could be about to follow. Latin America is experiencing more secure growth than it has in many years. The former planned economies of Europe are emerging from an economically disastrous half century. All are counting on being able to reap the benefits of international integration. By contrast, reduced birth rates and slow productivity growth have decreased potential growth throughout the developed world. If integration proceeds smoothly, the gains for the whole world will be enormous. If integration stalls and, even worse, if it reverses for whatever reason, the impact could be disastrous.

Scenario 3: Imperial Harmonization

The proverbial level playing field to which trade negotiators fondly refer is a cornerstone of most policy discussions. To some editorial writers and business executives and to many government officials the desirability of this objective seems obvious. But to foreigners this goal often sounds like insistence that they be "more like us." Makoto Kuroda, former vice minister of MITI, once remarked that he expected the day would come when he would be asked to take cornflakes instead of his favorite miso soup at breakfast as part of the next step toward the level playing field. The leveling process is in itself a political process whereby domestic structures, habits, and rules become the subject of comparisons, discussions, and not infrequently negotiations.

Thus in our third scenario, trade diplomacy would evolve toward more complex, more intrusive forms of harmonization. By contrast with the absence of government in a borderless world and the inward focus of policy under global fragmentation, our third scenario would entail a global, relatively open trading system that would result not from a spontaneous market-led process, as assumed under the invisible hand scenario, but from the assertion of economic and political power.

Key Actors

In this scenario the United States and the European Union would shape the world to their image. Lester Thurow has argued that the world will break into three blocs around the United States, Europe, and Japan.[12] In our view, however, for the next couple of decades only the United States and the European Union could exercise the carrot-and-stick diplomacy associated with imperial harmonization.

The U.S. market is an essential outlet for all major participants on the international economic scene. The United States composes roughly half the world market in high-technology or high-value-added sectors. The disproportionate presence of U.S. businesses among leading edge customers—companies with the most demanding expectations with respect to their suppliers—further intensifies the desires of businesses to be active in the U.S. market.[13]

At the other end of the economic spectrum, developing economies also depend heavily on the U.S. market, particularly in the first stages of their growth. The U.S. market is more open to manufactured imports than are those of most other nations, and U.S. corporations are more inclined to invest in developing countries as part of a global production strategy than are companies located elsewhere.

The importance of the U.S. market reinforces the tendency of Americans to view their practices as the ones others should emulate. The result is a U.S. assertion of extraterritoriality and a willingness to apply countervailing actions when foreign actions differ from what is desired. Extraterritoriality is apparent in environmental protection norms, disclosure rules, and regulatory definitions. The United States is prepared to use countervailing measures to offset foreign advantages perceived as unfair.

12. Thurow (1992).
13. Porter (1990).

The European Union will increasingly find itself tempted to take an extraterritorial approach. The European market is larger though less integrated and, in some respects, less technically advanced than the U.S. market. The bargaining power of the European Union approximates that of the United States in intermediary products and many consumer goods, if not in high-technology products. Some European countries and, on occasion, the European Commission have used Europewide public procurement and R&D consortia to help European insiders. European approaches differ substantially from U.S. ones; for instance, European competition policy invokes job maintenance and creation and the integration of internal markets in determining acceptable business practices.

The Scenario

A world of imperial harmonization would contain four elements. The United States and the European Union would be at the hubs of regional blocs, with a Pacific zone less integrated than the United States or Europe but their equal in trade. Relations among the three groups would display conflict and acrimony. Accordingly, they would rely on the fourth element, a multilateral system, to avoid breakdown.

TWO HUBS. The United States would apply its norms and procedures extraterritorially, reviewing and analyzing foreign practices and structures with such instruments as Super 301 and negotiations patterned after the U.S.-Japanese structural impediments initiatives. The United States would involve itself in policies of other nations affecting the environment, corporate practices, competition law, workers' rights, wages, and other labor standards. In return, it would offer partner countries specific trade and investment benefits and a framework in which to identify and settle the conflicts. Concessions such as those in NAFTA would be the carrot, while Super 301 and negotiations similar to the U.S.-Japan negotiations over strategic impediments would be the stick.

In such an environment the European Union would develop its own set of extraterritorial instruments with central and eastern European countries and Mediterranean countries. The French franc zone might negotiate membership in the European Monetary Union. The Union would grant development aid but insist on convergence to European norms and policies.

An implicit gentleman's agreement between the United States and the European Union would leave each free to police its own sphere. The current convergence of views between the United States and France on the need for the World Trade Organization to look at social dumping illustrates such cooperation.

Two hub-and-spoke networks of deeper integration agreements would emerge centered on the United States and the European Union. U.S. power would recall the era of gunboat trade diplomacy. The capacity by the United States to exempt its NAFTA-Plus partners from the legal harassment and uncertainties of its antitrust and other national remedies would increase the number of spokes around the U.S. hub. With fewer powers, Europe would be compelled to rely on incentives, made acceptable by contrast with the U.S. stick.

THE PACIFIC. Japan, China, and other Asian countries would resist imperial harmonization centered on the United States and Europe. Japanese negotiators would continue to give way on a limited number of issues and only after protracted negotiations. Japanese businesses would develop coalitions with foreign buyers to improve market shares, especially in other Asian countries worried about U.S. and European hegemony. However, Japan has neither the will nor the political capability to lead a cohesive integrated bloc, and many Asian countries resist deeper economic integration. Thus, far from emerging as a bloc, the Pacific economies would then constitute a third region of countries linked loosely with one another, united by aversion to intrusive rules required by the United States and Europe. The free-trade objective set up by the Asia-Pacific Economic Cooperation (APEC) forum in November 1994 would be implemented as a shallow integration agreement—dealing with trade and investments but not regulatory barriers.

In different ways Singapore and China illustrate a high readiness to trade combined with unwillingness to submit to foreign norms, values, and procedures. Malaysian resistance to a strong role for the Asia-Pacific Economic Cooperation and its preference for an East-Asian Economic Caucus (EAEC) excluding the United States, Canada, and Australia underscore the obstacles imperial harmonization would encounter in the Pacific region. The United States would push for NAFTA as a hemispheric counterpart to the "economic space" and association agreements put in place by the European Union and its neighboring countries, with respect notably to competition law, environment, and other aspects of regulatory convergence. Meanwhile, Europe would endeavor to involve the Mercosur countries (Brazil, Argentina, Uruguay, Paraguay) in a free trade zone patterned on the European rather than NAFTA model. More generally, interregional free trade agreements would develop in a rather antagonistic fashion and would test the borders of the two major hub-and-spoke trade regimes.

MULTILATERALISM OF LAST RESORT. The two blocs and the Pacific world would seek to maintain and even expand trade but would not seek deep integration among themselves. As a result of these actions, the function of multilateral institutions would be to prevent chaos rather than to create order and to contain trade wars rather than facilitate deep multilateral integration.

Key Issues

The most serious tensions would develop between these configurations. Capitalism versus capitalism would emerge as the successor to the cold war opposition between capitalism and communism.[14] Areas of tension would include corporate governance, technical norms, and regulatory barriers. The protection of shareholder rights from foreign challenges would justify technical and regulatory barriers. Diverse technical standards could serve not only as a source of higher innovation and competition but also as instruments of protection. With respect to regulatory barriers, governments would apply national treatment to the letter, with no element of mutual recognition, but might condition such treat-

14. Albert (1993); Hampden-Turner and Trompenaars (1993).

ment on the willingness of foreign companies to open their books and allow determination of whether they may have gained unfair advantages from operations in different regulatory environments. Using today's antidumping methodology would be a sure way to retain discretion in evaluation of these unfair advantages regarding, for instance, differences in environmental and social standards. European nations would erect protections needed to preserve their welfare systems. Privatization and Europewide deregulation would coexist, as would strong states, with a vigorous European Commission and new independent agencies.

Observations

None of these scenarios paints a picture of a world that is satisfactory. The notion advanced by advocates of the invisible hand that nation-states open to international trade and investment and acting in isolation can deal effectively with international interactions is questionable. The present state of integration has not been the fruit of benign neglect. Although private actors have often identified and addressed cross-border opportunities, government actions have been vital. Seven GATT rounds and government resistance to powerful lobbies have made trade liberalization and deregulation possible. To take recent examples, the French government has used the 1992 internal market to challenge vested interests and private monopolies that resisted international competition. Using national power and affiliation with GATT, Mexican president Salinas de Gortari dismantled tariffs running as high as 200 percent, engaged the United States in NAFTA negotiations, and submitted to codes of conduct established by the OECD. Without international guidance and cooperation, the liberal postwar order built around shallow integration could very well erode to the point where the other two scenarios would become more likely.

Economic, cultural, and political tensions could well produce global fragmentation. Tensions over labor rights, intellectual property, human rights, and environmental matters could derail economic integration. More generally, value conflicts could lead to a reassessment of the benefits of economic integration. The results would be devastating for the emerging economies.

Imperial harmonization stands as a plausible compromise between globalization and reaffirmation of national identities and national values. Two or three world power centers could compel other nations to adopt the standards and regulatory regimes of a few major economies. The result would be an open international system but one achieved at the expense of national diversity and autonomy. These scenarios inform the rest of this book, as we prescribe a balance among the forces behind them that combines their strengths but avoids their weaknesses.

Chapter 3

When Is International Cooperation Desirable?

THE WORLD is organized into sovereign nation-states. But under some circumstances nations can prosper by negotiating agreements that curb their own behavior or by creating international organizations with some powers of governance and coercion.

In chapter 1 we noted that the world has reduced trade barriers since World War II but retained national sovereignty for behind-the-border policies. We begin this chapter, therefore, by considering the case for shallow integration in which nations simply remove barriers to the mobility of goods, services, and factors of production but do not engage in extensive international cooperation beyond the minimum rules necessary to establish free trade.[1] If markets were complete and efficient and if political systems operated efficiently, this system would produce optimal results. However, some markets do not exist, some operate poorly, and political systems may fail to represent the interests of their citizens or to adhere to minimum standards of behavior.

Addressing the question of when some form of international cooperation or governance is necessary requires trade-offs among conflicting goals and is a fertile source of political tension. Nations may gain from deeper international integration if it allows them to internalize international spillovers, provide international public

---

1. Tinbergen (1954) drew a similar distinction between negative integration—the elimination of the barriers to the free movement of goods, services, and factors—and positive integration—the coordination and harmonization of policies.

goods, police opportunistic national actions, and take advantage of international economies of scale. But decentralized national decisionmaking can better accommodate diversity in national preferences and conditions, increase government accountability, and use common historical and cultural experiences to develop communal solidarity.

These considerations suggest that no single jurisdictional level is right for all types of governance. Instead, a multilevel approach is desirable, with the policy area dependent on the policy issue. For most policies, national or subnational approaches suffice. In some circumstances, however, the optimal jurisdiction may be larger than the nation-state.

Deciding on the appropriate jurisdiction requires prudent judgments about which reasonable observers may disagree. Before such judgments can be intelligently made, adequate knowledge and an information base are essential. The difficulty and sensitivity of these decisions suggest that piecemeal and functional solutions are preferable to the establishment of large, multifaceted organizational bureaucracies and that national autonomy should be preserved unless the arguments against it are overriding. In short, the case for subsidiarity, keeping governance as local as possible, is strong.

International cooperation can take various forms, ranging from consultation through coordination and harmonization to confederation. Each step entails a progressive loss of national independence and weakens political accountability. The reasons for making international control stronger should be progressively more solid as the associated loss of national sovereignty increases. Even where governance is international, national implementation should be maximized.

The Case for Shallow Integration

The theory of international trade demonstrates that a world organized into nation-states will maximize welfare by allowing free trade. This result stems from David Ricardo's insight that if costs differ internationally, countries can gain from free trade by exploiting their comparative advantage.[2]

In its conventional formulation, trade theory assumes the world is divided into nation-states, each with a given endowment of internationally immobile factors of production. Nations are sovereign and ignore other governments, with the exception of measures such as tariffs and quotas. Market-based determinants of costs, such as technology, tastes, and resources, cause national comparative advantage.

In reality, however, national governments' regulations, spending, and taxation shape resource allocation. These measures influence relative costs and thus help determine comparative advantage. The explanations for trade based on technology and relative factor endowments have been so widely invoked that the discovery that comparative advantage can actually be created by government action is sometimes treated as a major refutation of the principle of comparative advantage. However, Ricardo could as easily have ascribed the productive differences between nations to the social climate as to the physical climate and, given conditions we will elaborate later, his conclusions would have been unchanged: taking these climatic conditions as given, free trade will maximize global welfare. As long as government rules and spending are themselves set in a way that legitimately reflects local conditions and preferences, free trade will achieve a globally efficient distribution of resources.[3] Regulations and norms should reflect national conditions and preferences. Indeed, the more diverse these standards are, the larger the gains from trade. Participants in trade policy debates frequently claim to be seeking a level playing field. But as long as nations differ, competition between firms based in them can never be fair in the same way that

2. The necessary conditions for welfare maximization are stronger than Ricardo understood. As Kenneth Arrow and Gerard Debreu showed, markets in all commodities that enter utility or production functions must exist. This list includes markets for insurance against risk, which must not only exist but operate efficiently with complete and symmetric information.

3. Particular nations can gain from violating this maxim. The most notable theoretic example is the optimum tariff in which a nation can exploit its monopoly power to improve its terms of trade. For a general discussion of government intervention in the presence of market failure and its relationship to trade policy, see Johnson (1987).

competition between firms based in the same economy can be. If national tastes or conditions lead to different laws, the playing field of international competition will not, and should not, be level. Proposals advanced in the name of creating a level playing field—for example, tariffs on imported products to offset lower foreign costs or more lenient foreign regulation—would not only level the playing field but nullify the gains from trade. Traditional determinants of costs, such as relative factor endowments, technology, and tastes, should affect competitive performance, but so should regulations, institutions, and government policies.[4] Companies producing labor-intensive products should find it easy to operate in economies in which labor is abundant and cheap. Companies using pollution-intensive production methods should find it attractive to produce in economies with lenient pollution standards.

This conclusion does not, of course, imply that all groups in a country will benefit from the adoption of different rules and standards by their trading partners. Obviously, not all groups will find any given national policy attractive. If a country adopts relatively lenient pollution standards, at least two groups might object: producers in other countries with stricter standards that make pollution-intensive products and advocates of a clean environment in the country with lax standards. As long as standards reflect the outcome of a legitimate political process in each country, the outcome should improve aggregate welfare.

This view of trade, in which government actions influence comparative advantage, provides the rationale for the operating principles of the GATT-based system of international trade—what we call shallow integration. The essential elements in the system are free trade and national treatment. Nations should not distort trade by imposing border barriers, and they should treat foreign goods and domestic goods the same. Beyond these restraints, nations should be free to determine their domestic policies independently.

---

4. If markets are working perfectly, policy differences in one country may well put pressures on producers in others. But pressures that operate through the market do not signal market failure requiring government action.

The Case for Deeper Integration

If the conditions under which shallow integration maximizes global welfare are violated, international cooperation may improve economic outcomes. Two assumptions are of particular importance. The first is that markets are complete and competition is perfect. In particular, policies or production activities must not produce physical effects on people or businesses in other countries—so-called externalities or spillovers. The second condition is that nation-states legitimately reflect the interests of their citizens so that constraints need not be imposed on sovereign national choices, an assumption analogous to consumer sovereignty. If these conditions are violated, international action may be desirable.

Market Failures and Macroeconomic Spillovers

Market allocations can be efficient only if prices accurately reflect scarcity. Problems arise, therefore, when prices do not reflect activities that affect production and welfare.[5] The price system may fail to elicit sufficient production of public goods, products that additional businesses or people can use at no cost to anyone else. Markets also fail when one company can satisfy all market demand at lower production costs than can two or more companies—so-called natural monopolies. As long as these problems exist only within a single nation, there is no case for international action.[6]

Externalities, public goods, and economies of scale may also be international in scope. Examples include international pollution and environmental effects (acid rain and global warming, for example), public health measures (inadequate malarial control in one country can cause disease in others), research and development (science that produces freely available basic knowledge), and even national political decisions (war in Rwanda increases the

5. Baumol and Oates (1975).
6. Buiter and Kletzer (1992) point out that fiscal redistribution and changes in domestic budget policies may affect foreign welfare. But these pecuniary effects do not disturb allocative efficiency.

Box 3-1. Taxation and Mobility under Second-Best Conditions

Tax theorists sometimes assume that governments can raise revenues without distorting resource allocation by using lump-sum taxes. Nearly all actual taxes create significant domestic distortions, however. They do so by affecting labor supply, saving, consumer choices, and production decisions. Because consumers can avoid taxes by shopping abroad and capital can escape tax burdens by moving abroad, taxes create international distortions as well. Under these conditions, nations feel pressures to tax immobile factors and the consumption of goods that must be consumed domestically and to lower taxes on mobile factors. Eventually, owners of internationally mobile factors will be able to avoid paying for any government-financed goods and services that yield benefits to them that are of less value than the taxes they pay. Thus mobility erodes the capacity of national governments to redistribute income through transfers or public services.

In the presence of factor mobility, therefore, redistribution in one country creates spillovers in others. A costly solution to this problem is to prevent factor mobility. Alternatively, if people were immobile, nations could impose taxes on the basis of residence rather than source. Or nations could harmonize their tax systems to avoid spillovers or prevent mobile factors from escaping taxation. This example illustrates that unless policies are coordinated, pursuit of domestically justified tax policies could actually reduce national welfare when factors of production are internationally mobile. Similar observations apply to such regulations as clean air standards, banking regulation, and workplace safety rules.

---

number of immigrants to Zaire). Some resources belong to the world at large, including the deep seabed, the broadcast spectrum, and the atmosphere. Assignment of property rights or joint management is crucial to prevent overexploitation of such resources. In all these cases, international agreement could be required to obtain a mechanism to ensure optimal global supply (box 3–1).

MONOPOLY POWER. A nation with international market power can in principle increase its welfare at the expense of others by using a tariff to improve its terms of trade. By imposing an import tariff, for example, a large nation could drive down the world price of its imports. This cost saving to that nation could more than offset tariff-induced efficiency losses. Domestic policies can replicate the effects of such a tariff. For example, domestic excise taxes on commodities that are normally imported produce effects similar to tariffs. Other domestic policies may not only promote domestic regulatory goals but also enhance terms of trade. For example, the South African government might agree not to tax gold exports, but could impose high worker safety standards (or production taxes) in its gold mines, thereby limiting the supply and thus raising the world price of a major export. Similarly, a government in a major oil-importing nation could use excessively stringent environmental regulations to limit oil demand, lower world oil prices, and improve its terms of trade. As strategic trade theory shows, nations can increase the rents earned by national companies and workers by using subsidies to drive foreign firms out of imperfectly competitive international markets.[7] If countries use domestic rules and subsidies to shift the terms of trade, international action may be required to constrain them. But international action could provide an even greater opportunity for abuse: if all gold producers jointly stiffened mine safety standards, for instance, or if all oil-importing nations implemented stringent environmental regulations, or if nations producing pollution control equipment persuaded all nations to mandate the use of such equipment.

Regulatory harmonization can reduce factors that render competition imperfect. Recent trade theory shows that trade can occur between countries with identical environments if products are differentiated, consumers have a taste for variety, and there are scale economies in production.[8] The United States may sell IBM computers to Japan while Japan sells Fujitsu computers in the United States. If standards are such that the products of these companies compete directly with one another, the demand facing any single producer becomes more elastic. As a result, producers will increase output and lower costs.

Divergent government regulations may increase the costs of market entry for foreign producers and preserve international market segmentation. When the U.S. dollar was strong, for example, foreign auto producers could charge higher prices in the

7. Brander and Spencer (1985).
8. Helpman and Krugman (1985).

United States than abroad because regulatory differences prevented the cars bought outside the United States from being
driven without costly changes. Under these conditions, the re-
moval of barriers that permit market segmentation may yield
important welfare benefits.[9] The benefits to be derived from the
increased competition stimulated by harmonizing regulatory standards should be balanced against the costs of having standards
that may ignore diverse consumer tastes.

DOMESTIC DISTORTIONS: SECOND-BEST CONSIDERATIONS. Free trade
improves resource allocation when domestic markets are free of
distortions. So does international factor mobility, but not if there
are serious domestic market failures. If domestic prices do not
correctly reflect value, free trade can actually push a country away
from allocative efficiency. Assume, for example, that a nation has a
strong comparative advantage in producing steel, but that a strong
labor union pushes up the costs of producing it. Free trade might
drive the nation out of the steel industry entirely. Protection
might preserve at least some steel production, an outcome that
is closer to the optimal result. The first-best solution is to have
labor accurately priced. If this condition is not satisfied and other
policy measures are precluded, trade intervention may improve
results. For analogous reasons, international coordination may be
preferable to independent action.

Our consideration of market failures leads to a commonsense
principle: the domain of jurisdiction should correspond to the
domain of the direct effects of actions on welfare and production.
Where spillovers are local or national, local or national government can fully deal with them. Where spillovers are international,
international action may be needed.

Similarly, the scope of scale economies in providing private and
public goods is important in determining the jurisdictional level at
which they should be managed. International action may be desirable
to restrict large economies from exploiting market power and to deter
companies from using product standards to segment markets.

9. Absent full market integration, imperfectly competitive companies have incentives to
engage in price discrimination and so-called reciprocal dumping. See Brander and Spencer
(1985).

MACROECONOMIC SPILLOVERS. In open economies where national policies affect conditions in other nations, cooperative solutions may achieve better results than noncooperative ones. Most nations worry about trade deficits. These fears could cause policymakers to restrict demand. The result could be less economic activity than would occur if all nations expanded simultaneously. Similarly, under flexible exchange rates, nations might pursue policies to appreciate their currencies, thereby shifting inflationary risks to other nations. Or they might seek to depreciate their currencies to maintain domestic demand. By coordinating their policies, nations may be able to achieve superior outcomes, although problems of coordination are serious (box 3–2).[10]

Political Failures

With the exception of the recurring assertion by one or another nation of the right to protect nationals residing in foreign jurisdictions, the principle that how nation-states treat their subjects is a purely domestic matter has been accepted doctrine in international relations at least since the Treaty of Westphalia in 1648. But the conditions that have created pressures for deeper economic integration and integration itself test this principle severely. First, increasing economic openness exposes domestic policies to foreign scrutiny because such policies affect foreigners and because open communication makes governments' misdeeds against their own citizens visible throughout the world. Second, countries themselves use various rules to prevent policy from moving instantly to comply with possibly evanescent sentiments of the majority. Treaty obligations and foreign pressures can support constitutional provisions designed to ensure that governmental policies reflect enduring convictions.

REPRESENTATION AND SHARED VALUES. The principle that governments are legitimate if they accurately represent the views and interests of their citizens resembles the market principle that markets are functioning well only if they represent the tastes and preferences of those who operate within them. The basic assump-

10. Bryant (1995).

Box 3-2. Optimal Currency Areas

What is an optimal currency area? Permanently fixed exchange rates or a common currency reduce transaction costs by creating certainty and eliminating the need to convert one currency into another. On these grounds, a single global currency is most efficient.[a]

Efficiency in exchange is not the only consideration associated with the choice of currency, however. National economies are subject to a variety of shocks that destabilize employment and prices. The optimal region for macroeconomic policy depends on the nature of the disturbances. If domestic disturbances are small, an isolated economy will be more stable than one closely integrated into the world economy. If domestic shocks are large, an integrated economy will be more stable than an isolated one because the shocks can spill over into the rest of the world. The extent to which domestic and external shocks are correlated is also important. If they are inversely related, economies will benefit from integration and risk pooling. If they are correlated, however, economies could become less stable with increased integration.

A second set of considerations relates to the efficiency of market adjustments to such disturbances. If factors are mobile, adjustment will tend to occur smoothly.[b] This line of argument suggests that the appropriate domain for policy corresponds to that of factor (particularly labor) mobility. Similarly, if prices and wages are flexible, adjustment to disturbances will proceed easily. Exchange rate flexibility may be another mechanism for achieving such flexibility, suggesting that, particularly in the presence of rigid nominal wages and prices, exchange rate areas should be fairly small. However, extremely small and open economies may actually derive little benefit from exchange rate flexibility because in very open economies, there is little money illusion, so that wages and prices tend to rapidly offset such changes.[c]

A third set of considerations relates to the effectiveness of policy. Nations will typically try to use macroeconomic policies to offset disturbances. For small open economies, however, the more integrated their goods, capital, and labor markets are with the rest of world, the less effective such policies will be. Indeed, if exchange rates are fixed and capital mobile, a nation cannot set monetary policy independently because interest rates are determined internationally. In this situation, nations have to accept internationally determined inflation rates and monetary conditions. In principle, fiscal policy can be used for stabilization, but the more open the economy, the larger the spillovers into the rest of the world. In a floating exchange rate system, individual nations can in principle regain control over their monetary policy, but in the short run both domestic and foreign monetary shocks will affect the exchange rate and thus real domestic activity unless wages and prices are perfectly flexible.

a. Because nations that issue money enjoy benefits from seigniorage, some method of dividing up these gains would be required.
b. Mundell (1961).
c. McKinnon (1963).

tion behind shallow integration is that the values and preferences of nations (or citizens), as embodied in their economic policies, in general should not be constrained. Under this view, inalienable international rights that all nations must respect do not exist. The legitimate scrutiny of foreigners ends at national borders.

However, rigid adherence to this principle of international relations may be questioned. Markets fail when they do not accurately represent consumer preferences. In much the same sense, political systems can be said to fail if they grossly misrepresent the views or violate the interests of their citizens. Judging when such abuses arise is subtle and difficult. No political system can always accurately represent the views and interests of the population.[11] Furthermore, many government officials see themselves as representative not only of today's voters but of a cultural tradition. And intensity of preferences or interests in political outcomes frequently influences decisions, as it should.

In extreme cases, however, political systems disenfranchise or exploit their citizens in egregious ways. In such cases, other nations participating in an integrated world economy may complain of what they see as affronts to common decency. The fact that products produced under repressive conditions may supplant the exports of other nations can only add to this sense of outrage.

We believe that the principle of subsidiarity, which should apply in international relations if deeper integration is to prove sustainable, can also be applied to domestic affairs of nations. Because tastes vary, governments should delegate responsibility to levels of government within which people have relatively similar tastes. Such a policy increases the likelihood that governments will produce the kinds and amounts of public services people want.

Deeper integration will require international mechanisms, acceptable to nation-states, that can take action when governments grossly violate their duty to represent the views and interests of their citizens. Because alleged violator governments always resent foreign interference and because evidence of political failure as we

---

11. Indeed, Kenneth Arrow proved, with his impossibility theorem, that a democratic process such as majority rule may be incapable of accurately aggregating diverse individual preferences into a consistent collective set of preferences.

define that term is so seldom clear beyond a reasonable doubt, foreign actions must be measured and restrained.

Various examples illustrate how legitimate assertion of domestic preferences can raise knotty problems in an open world economy. French, Canadian, and other governments refuse to accept the verdict of an open market if it means that their own citizens prefer foreign—usually American—cultural expression to their own. Although traditional financial motives may lie behind such protection, a legitimate case can be made that a nation's culture is a public good and that markets fail in general to produce adequate quantities of public goods. Another example is the family farm, valued in many countries for reasons that go well beyond these farms' ability to compete in the market. Under such circumstances, nations will and should promote these activities. The key is to do so in the most precise and efficient manner possible, in particular through direct subsidies rather than trade policies. Even subsidies, however, are certain to provoke controversy among trading partners. The solution is international negotiation within frameworks we shall sketch in the next chapter.

In other cases, governments may express their preferences but nonetheless affront foreigners. The most notable example in recent history was the South African policy of apartheid. Less extreme instances involve cruelty to animals. A much more controversial example is the U.S. contention that the government of China exploits prison labor and exports products made by such labor. Policies in poor countries, such as child labor or a lack of pollution controls, can offend the sensibilities of those in rich nations. Under all such circumstances outsiders can suffer what Richard Cooper has characterized as "psychological externalities."[12]

Where abhorrent practices reflect poverty rather than differences in values, the long-run solution is to increase incomes in offending countries. In the short run, however, explicit subsidies may help.[13] For example, the European Union has social funds that allow poorer countries to meet the labor and social standards applied by more affluent members. Similarly, so-called debt-for-

12. Cooper (1994).
13. Collins (forthcoming).

nature swaps allow rich nations to support environmental protection in poor countries. In other cases, countries may trade changes of particular practices for concessions in other areas. In the Uruguay Round, for example, some developing countries agreed to introduce rules to protect intellectual property in return for increased access to markets for their textiles and agricultural products.

Sometimes divergent practices reflect strong divergent beliefs, and a compensatory trade-off is impossible. Under these circumstances, those who believe that certain values should be universal may not accept the results of shallow integration. Nonetheless, efforts to impose certain values, even those of the majority, on others should be viewed with considerable suspicion, particularly in a diverse global community. Such attempts are especially problematic when those who demand that other countries meet particular standards—clean air, for example—do not have to pay the costs.

TIME, CONSISTENCY, AND CREDIBILITY. Many nations establish procedures to prevent governments from responding quickly to the sentiments of the majority. International cooperation can support such restraints when instantaneous accountability is not preferred. Some nations have constitutional constraints to prevent narrow majorities from acting. Many have one legislative branch that is not popularly elected (the British House of Lords, for example) or whose members have relatively lengthy terms of office (the U.S. Senate).

Nations also use international agreements with penalties for withdrawal to constrain domestic policies. Nations have, for example, tried to strengthen their anti-inflationary resolve by pegging their currencies. Similarly, the desire to support democratic institutions contributed to the decisions by Portugal, Spain, and Greece to join the European Community, and the goal of strengthening commitments to trade liberalization played a part in the decision by Mexico to join NAFTA. In the context of macroeconomic policies, nations sometimes adhere to rules for fiscal or monetary policy rather than give authorities continuous discretion. Systems of international rules provide benefits even to the most powerful nations by protecting them from short-sighted demands of constituents. Although strong nations may prevail under disorderly anarchy, they typically can do even better under stable order.

Implications

When should nations cooperate? Many considerations affect the answer. They include the jurisdictional scope required to correct market failures, internalize the costs and benefits of policies, and achieve redistribution; the technology of producing regulations and public goods efficiently; the correlation of economic disturbances among nations; the pattern and intensities of values and preferences; and the legitimacy of claims about fundamental values.

Some considerations point to more decentralized governance than exists today, including variability of tastes, the desirability of ensuring accountability, and the gains from jurisdictional competition. However, other considerations, such as macroeconomic spillovers, efficient supply of international public goods, and international externalities, point to more centralized governance.

The jurisdictional rules of shallow integration have great merit in a pluralistic world. They facilitate trade while allowing diversity. They allow for a close matching between policies, preferences, and costs. They promote accountability of governments for local concerns. They encourage regulatory experimentation and competition. Shallow integration will not suffice, however, where spillovers are international, where redistribution is important, and where the benefits of international economies of scale and increased international competition outweigh those of national diversity. The cases where national values conflict and domestic public choice mechanisms are viewed as illegitimate are particularly difficult.

Although full national autonomy may be inadequate, centralized global government is impractical and undesirable. The future success of international economic relations will hinge on finding acceptable intermediate solutions. We have laid out conceptually the problems in the current world economy to which deeper international integration is an answer. We have also pointed to the problems that deeper integration will provoke.

Deeper integration will allow nations to internalize international spillovers, provide international public goods, police opportunistic national actions, and take advantage of international scale economies. But decentralized national decisionmaking accommodates diversity in national preferences and conditions, facilitates governmental accountability, and is an effective mechanism for giving voice to common historical and cultural experiences in developing communal solidarity. In each policy area, judgments need to be made about the relative weights of these considerations. It is important to stress, therefore, that more international cooperation is not necessarily better than less.

The relative weights these considerations should enjoy differs by place and topic. Because of the complexity and sensitivity of these goals, we urge piecemeal and functional solutions wherever possible, rather than emphasize the creation of large, multifaceted organizational bureaucracies, and the preservation of national autonomy unless arguments against it are overriding. International cooperation can take various forms, ranging from consultation to confederation, with coordination and harmonization in between. The greater the loss of national independence, the stronger must be the case for the surrender of autonomy.

These considerations suggest that there is no ideal jurisdictional level for all governance. For the most part, the benefits from free trade and investment should not be abridged. At the same time, varied national circumstances and preferences suggest that under many circumstances different institutions and rules are desirable. However, when markets and national governments fail, some measure of international governance should be considered.

Chapter 4

The Vision

THE SCENARIOS described earlier are plausible alternative futures for the world economy. None is ideal. It would be desirable to avoid the dangers of global fragmentation by keeping nations open, while at the same time achieving the diversity of the invisible hand and more equitable international governance than is likely under imperial harmonization. In short, the desirable outcome means a world marked by openness, diversity, and cohesion. Openness increases competition and limits monopoly power. Diversity accommodates different national conditions and preferences and allows for experimentation and innovation. Trust in the institutions and practices of other nations and in international institutions is essential if increased openness is to be viable and diversity tolerated.

How might these goals be realized? We turn now from analysis to prescription, presenting a vision of the world not as it is, but as it might be. Some of the steps needed to realize this vision must be taken over the next decade, but many will take much longer.

A Global Community

A global community must be open, diverse, and cohesive. We stress each word of this goal. *Openness* requires that nations avoid the use of domestic policies or strategic trade policies to exclude foreign goods or investments at home or to gain unfair advantage abroad. New institutions and agreements are necessary to ensure that domestic policies and practices allow foreign products, services, and companies to compete fully in domestic markets. This goal requires transparent domestic practices and contestable domestic markets. *Diversity* requires international policies that accommodate differences in national conditions, preferences, and traditions. Nations must be free to experiment and to innovate. We specifically reject the prescription of identical national policies and practices—the strictly level playing field. *Cohesion* requires a community held together by trust, mutual respect, shared basic values, and, where necessary, shared governance and elements of redistribution. To increase openness and acceptance of diversity, nations must come to trust values, practices, and institutions of other nations and accept the role of international institutions.

None of these three elements should be sacrificed to the others. For example, extreme openness could be achieved by eliminating diversity and enforcing uniformity. Allowing diversity to dominate could undermine openness and cohesion. Similarly, enforcing cohesion in a strictly level playing field could limit innovation and diversity. The key is a balance in a fashion similar to the ideals of the French Revolution—liberty, equality, and fraternity.

As an American, a European, and a Japanese, we believe that each of our societies offers essential ingredients for realizing this vision. From America, the most open society, we take the lesson of transparency and an open system based on rules. From Europe, the most diverse, we take the principles of mutual recognition and subsidiarity. From Japan, the most cohesive of our countries, we take the principle of cooperation based on trust and consensus.

Transparency and Rules

The U.S. system of government is more transparent than those of most other countries. Transparency is necessary in a geographically large and culturally diverse democracy. The United States relies less markedly than do most nations on the assumption of tacitly shared norms and values. The states have therefore enshrined their principles in a national constitution and system of laws. Strong reliance on a written constitution makes the rules of the game clearer than they are in nations where commonly shared traditions supplant reliance on formal rules. The United States also uses rules to keep the society open. Laws ban discrimination on the grounds of age, race, or gender and extend these protections to both citizens and aliens. In many areas affirmative action has been used to redress the historical effects of discrimination.

The United States uses transparency, legal controls, and strict standards of legal due process to limit government power. The Constitution and Bill of Rights express a deeply rooted mistrust of concentrated power and of bureaucratic discretion. The legislative process features open congressional hearings to solicit diverse views. Before promulgation, regulations are published in the *Federal Register* and comments from all interested parties are invited. Once in force, laws and regulations are subject to judicial challenge and review. Not only does the Bill of Rights protect free speech and a free press, but the courts sedulously enforce these rights. Ordinary citizens enjoy access to government information under the Freedom of Information Act to an extent available in few other nations. Citizens and foreigners alike can buy political intelligence, access, and influence by hiring professional lobbyists.

Many other nations employ different procedures to run themselves. Bureaucrats enjoy much greater discretion. They can tailor decisions flexibly to new and different circumstances, but decisions are often unclear to outsiders and abuse of power is harder to detect and more difficult to punish. But to be open, national economies need transparent systems based on clear rules and enforcement procedures. Openness also increases access to information that is vital for almost every aspect of deeper integration. Information is necessary so that foreign companies and individuals not only enjoy nondiscriminatory access (national treatment) but also understand that they enjoy equal treatment. Procedures marked by bureaucratic discretion are easily captured by insiders and difficult for outsiders to penetrate.

Mutual Recognition and Subsidiarity

The European Community has gradually moved beyond national treatment and relied increasingly on the principle of mutual recognition of national regulations, standards, and authorizations.

This practice grew out of the realization that national treatment was insufficient for a single market but complete harmonization was also undesirable. First, unanimity among all partners is often impossible to achieve. Second, uniformity is undesirable because identical rules may fail to meet diverse local needs. Accordingly, the European Community decided to apply the principle of mutual recognition where agreed standards did not exist. In fact, mutual recognition may actually require more trust than harmonization does because each nation retains wide discretion. Mutual recognition looks simple, but its reality is complex.

Opponents of mutual recognition claim that it will lead to the debasement of regulatory standards. They fear that integrated international markets are incompatible with high but diverse standards. In fact, consumers are prepared to pay more for products that meet strict standards. Investors accept lower rates of return when companies and financial institutions are safe. Workers are more productive and accept lower wages when they are involved in decisionmaking and when workplaces are safe and healthful. And taxpayers grouse less about high taxes when government services satisfy popular wants. Nor will mutual recognition result inexorably in uniform rules and procedures. Large, open, and competitive markets typically feature more variation and choice than do small, closely regulated markets. In competitive markets, to be sure, a best or dominant practice or product will drive out inferior ones. The same would be true under mutual recognition. But the market will support diversity if it meets real needs.

For example, if residents of one nation prefer safer consumer products and workplaces or superior education, health care, or other public services, their political systems can implement these preferences and sustain them. For all these reasons, mutual recognition can best achieve diversity and openness in most situations.

There are two important exceptions. First, when regulations are used for redistributive purposes, international cooperation can reduce the burdens redistribution places on immobile factors of production. Second, agreed minimum standards rather than mutual recognition may be required to resolve problems whose scope is international such as global environmental problems.

The European experience has also shown that not all issues require international governance. Indeed, the Maastricht Treaty holds that only compelling reasons for cooperation can overcome the presumption that local governance is preferable. Article 3b of the Treaty Establishing the European Community enshrines this subsidiarity principle.

"In areas which do not fall within its exclusive competence, the Community shall take action, in accordance with the principle of subsidiarity, only if and insofar as the objectives of the proposed action cannot be sufficiently achieved by the Member States and can therefore, by reason of the scale or effects of the proposed action, be better achieved by the Community."

This policy requires those who would centralize to demonstrate that the benefits from coordination outweigh its costs.[1]

Consensus and Trust

Long-term cooperation among equals requires a measure of trust. Confrontational negotiations are incompatible with the establishment and maintenance of such trust.

Japan has used consensus-building deliberation councils extensively. They are often slow, and critics charge that they give too much weight to vested interests. But consensus building has resulted in gradual and stable changes. In particular, government decisions do not flip-flop, and most hostile feelings are mollified before decisions are made. Stable international relations require institutions similar to Japanese councils for building consensus. Before the GATT negotiations on services and agriculture, for example, considerable discussion took place in the OECD. Currently, similar deliberations have begun on competition policy. To be sure, these deliberations did not eliminate hard bargaining. Advance negotiations—sometimes confrontational—among the United States, Japan, and the European Community played a vital role in the successful conclusion of the Uruguay Round. Because signatories to a treaty usually have equal votes, consensus building will be critical.

1. Centre for Economic Policy Research (1993).

Trust is also important after a treaty has been signed. Treaties cannot address all contingencies. Mutual understanding of the spirit, as well as the letter, of rules is vital. When disputes occur, multilateral mediation and arbitration by entities such as the World Trade Organization should be used whenever possible. Unilateral actions have two principal defects. Domestic interests can more readily capture such initiatives, and unilateral actions can erode the trust of those who are accused. By contrast, impartial arbitration imposes an external discipline on opportunistic behavior and allows resolution based on substance rather than power or force. Trust is crucial when responsibilities are assigned to international agencies. Accountability and legitimacy require that such organizations operate with efficiency, competence, and transparency.

Next Steps: A World of Clubs

The practical problem concerns *how* to establish and maintain openness, diversity, and consensus. International integration allows nations to internalize international spillovers, provide international public goods, police opportunistic national actions, and take advantage of international economies of scale. Decentralized national decisionmaking permits the exercise of diverse national preferences and conditions, makes government accountable, maintains diversity when no policy is demonstrably superior to all others, and sustains political systems rooted in common historical and cultural experiences.

In each policy area, judgments must be made about the relative importance of these considerations. Although a single global government is unlikely, these conflicts also suggest that it is undesirable. A global federation could, in principle, realize the efficiency benefits from integrated markets and also undertake international redistribution. But it would reduce political accountability, lack political legitimacy, and stifle beneficial diversity. Consequently, the nation-state will continue to be the fundamental global political unit. The European Union is a possible exception, although, as William Wallace has noted, despite its achievements, Europe does not yet really have a popularly accepted new political system.[2] For this reason international cooperation must focus on issues rather than creating large bureaucracies and institutions. Furthermore, as nations consider greater limits on their sovereignty, the case for moving forward should be progressively stronger.

We refer to the international agreements and organizations that deal with particular issues or that link groups of nations as clubs. We choose this term because clubs are voluntary associations of willing members who combine to achieve shared objectives. We distinguish three types of clubs. Functional clubs address single issues. Regional clubs deal with several functional areas for groups of countries. The system should also be steered by coordinating institutions that oversee several issue areas—the club of clubs. Together these three tiers form a world of clubs.

Many international organizations and arrangements currently operate as clubs in the sense that we use the term, although not all follow the procedures we advocate. These include GATT, the International Monetary Fund, the Bank for International Settlements, the Organization for Economic Cooperation and Development, and the European Union. New clubs should expand this roster.

General Principles

Clubs establish rights and duties of their members based on shared values and mutual benefits, not coercion.[3] They are generally concerned with collective goods, allowing members to realize scale economies. They reduce free ridership by excluding non-members from club benefits. Membership may be open to all who agree to abide by club rules and to honor club obligations or may require approval of current members.

In our view, international functional clubs and the overarching club of clubs should be open to all nations prepared to abide by the conditions of membership. Wherever possible, regional clubs should also be open, although approval by current members may be

2. Wallace (1994).
3. Cornes and Sandler (1986).

necessary when clubs seek particularly extensive coordination or are precursors to new federal systems. Overlaps and multiple memberships by nations in clubs are essential in achieving an open global environment.

Clubs should have several common features. *To achieve transparency,* they should institutionalize international information sharing, frequent exchanges between officials, and open and transparent systems for determining and enforcing rules. Clubs should also include arrangements to allow for the participation and advice of nongovernmental organizations and associations. *To ensure diversity,* subsidiarity should be honored so that international governance is used only when strictly necessary. For example, members should be free to choose how to achieve agreed standards. Wherever possible, beyond adherence to minimum standards, countries could grant one another mutual recognition. Similarly, clubs should entrust implementation to national authorities wherever possible and forgo large institutionalized bureaucracies. *To bolster cohesion,* decisions should usually be based on consensus. Exceptions could be made when members make disproportionate contributions to club resources or when less developed countries require extended transitional periods to meet club obligations. Clubs should also emphasize technical and financial assistance to developing countries seeking to upgrade their capacity to meet club norms. To make commitments credible, clubs should establish binding enforcement mechanisms, immune to the veto power of the country under review.

New Clubs

Many functional clubs exist, although not all conform to all these features. The clubs include, for example, the Bank for International Settlements, the International Labor Organization, and the United Nations Environment Program.[4] More functional clubs

---

4. Regional clubs include the European Union, the North American Free Trade Agreement, and the Asia-Pacific Economic Cooperation forum. Some overarching clubs exist as well: the United Nations, the World Trade Organization, and the Organization for Economic Cooperation and Development.

are necessary to ensure internationally contestable markets, promote international technology development, and maintain the global environment. Although they may necessitate controversial constraints on international sovereignty, clubs for international taxation and macroeconomic coordination also merit consideration.

Competition

A new club is needed to ensure that international markets are open and competitive. The club could be independent or part of the World Trade Organization, although it would probably not initially include all WTO members. The club would deal with issues of competition policy, foreign investment, government regulation, corporate governance, and product standards. Members would no longer apply the current trade rules allowing subsidies and preventing dumping. Instead, competition policies would define fair trade. Club members would agree to an enforceable code of conduct for domestic regulatory practices and subsidies. They would guarantee foreign companies full national treatment, including access to government procurement contracts and participation in government-sponsored technology consortia. The club would require mutual recognition of differing forms of corporate governance, actively monitor standards and regulatory practices in member countries, and ensure for exporters the ability to secure certification of foreign standards in their home country.

DUMPING. GATT rules on dumping and subsidies embody the shallow integration approach to achieving fair international competition. At the same time, antitrust or other regulatory policies promote fair domestic competition. A new organization or club should seek to establish basic rules of competition policy and credible means of enforcement to replace current rules on dumping and subsidies.

Current dumping rules are defective, in part because the coexistence of different international and domestic rules for fair trade results in inconsistent and inequitable treatment for domestic and foreign companies. Companies that charge prices abroad that are lower than their domestic prices or that set prices below average cost are guilty of dumping under GATT. If either form of pricing causes injury, an offsetting duty may be assessed on the company's foreign sales.

But what is the unfairness these rules are designed to offset? One answer might be the implicit subsidy that a monopoly position at home provides for sales abroad. However, the solution applied—a compensating duty—does not deal with the source of the problem—the closed foreign market that allows the foreign company to maintain its domestic monopoly. An alternative answer is that the foreign company is behaving in a predatory fashion. But the country imposing the penalty need not show predation. Selling below marginal cost might constitute evidence of predation. However, dumping is defined as selling below average cost, although such behavior may be appropriate business strategy, particularly when a company has excess capacity or enters a new market. Furthermore companies may rationally let profit margins fall rather than raise prices in the face of currency fluctuations or other changes in market conditions thought to be temporary.

Moreover, antidumping pricing rules do not apply to domestic companies. A foreign exporter can be found guilty of dumping even when it has the same costs and prices as its domestic competitors. Domestic companies can use the dumping rules to harass importers and facilitate their own collusion. A single regime for competition policy would avoid these inequities.

International competition policies are required for other reasons. GATT rules restrict export sales when prices are too low, not when they are too high. The rules do nothing to curtail abusive behavior by cartels or monopolies. Many nations actually exempt domestic exporters from antitrust rules.[5] Indeed, governments often instruct their domestic companies to join international cartels or voluntary restraint arrangements, thereby allowing companies that might otherwise face prosecution by the antitrust authorities in their export markets to claim immunity based on sovereign compulsion.

No authority today carries the responsibility to ensure that global markets remain competitive. As a result, nations fall prey to

5. Scherer (1994).

such practices or they resort to industrial policies to limit their vulnerability. Developing countries in particular have expressed concern in the United Nations about such practices. The result has been a suggested Code of Conduct for Multinational Corporations. Europeans justify government subsidies to Airbus Industrie, for example, by claiming that without such subsidies, Europe would be vulnerable to Boeing's dominant global position. Similarly, U.S. advocates of Sematech claimed that U.S. government and private collaboration was needed to reduce the monopoly power of Japanese producers of semiconductor equipment.

An international agreement not to use domestic law to enforce international cartel agreements would be a minimal approach to the cartel issue.[6] The American Bar Association has recommended instead that countries repeal laws granting immunity to export cartels and prosecute cartel conduct at home and in the export market.

Both steps are useful, but F. M. Scherer has suggested a more ambitious approach. He proposes creation of an International Competition Policy Office that would gather information, investigate anticompetitive behavior, and authorize aggrieved nations to take appropriately graduated countermeasures (such as the exercise of extraterritorial jurisdiction by national courts).[7] Scherer emphasizes the importance of proceeding simultaneously with both cartel and merger policies. All cartels and companies with large shares of world export markets would register with the ICPO. Later all companies planning to merge would also have to register. Nations that think trade has been restrained could petition the ICPO for redress. Initially, the office would cooperate with local authorities and recommend actions. Later it would be given power to intervene in cases with serious implications for global markets.

The ICPO would encourage domestic authorities to deal with most cases independently. It might, however, form international panels to arbitrate cases where parties claimed that others had violated internationally agreed norms or that domestic laws had

6. Scherer (1994).
7. Scherer (1994, pp. 92–95).

not been adequately enforced. NAFTA mechanisms for handling appeals on national trade rules are similar.

One element of current antidumping laws could be used extensively by the ICPO. Large price differentials between markets are key indicators of entry and arbitrage barriers. The International Competition Office should collect data on price differentials, investigate why they arise, and propose or enforce measures to narrow them. The price differential test currently used to detect dumping should be maintained. Either consumer interests in the home country or the international antitrust authority would bring price discrimination cases. In contrast to current remedies, companies judged guilty of dumping should be required to lower their higher domestic prices, not to raise their foreign prices or face tariffs.

SUBSIDIES. The ICPO should also police subsidies and state aid. GATT recognizes subsidies as legitimate instruments for promotion of social and economic policy objectives. The Uruguay Round groups these measures into three categories: red, or prohibited; yellow, or permissible but countervailable if they cause adverse trade effects; and green, or nonactionable and noncountervailable, provided they are structured according to criteria to limit trade distortion. National views remain divided, however, on the legitimacy of subsidies for industrial restructuring and on subsidies that directly affect the competitiveness of companies. Subsidies to aid displaced workers and those to promote research and development should be allowed. Those directed at increasing the capacity or sustaining the operation of companies should be eliminated. Member countries would be required to submit data on their subsidies to the ICPO for review. Even before a group such as the ICPO is formed, we advocate measures to increase transparency by establishing or strengthening review processes and discussions in forums such as the OECD and increasing the number of agreements regulating specific subsidies, such as those for shipbuilding and civilian aircraft.

NATIONAL TREATMENT. For markets to function properly, new companies must be able to enter them. When global markets are fragmented, nations are tempted to use their domestic policies to exploit their monopoly power. One antidote to such policies is to ensure that domestic markets are competitive and open to foreign investment and trade. The agreement in the Uruguay Round that prohibits trade-distorting measures such as local content and export performance requirements represents only a minimal first step because it concentrates only on measures that distort trade. It does not guarantee rights of establishment and full national treatment. Similarly, the new agreement in the Uruguay Round to liberalize services—the General Agreement on Trade in Services, or GATS—applies only to selected sectors and measures.[8] The ICPO, by contrast, would promote market access and national treatment for all trade and investment, with no sectoral exceptions.

Many policymakers and economists believe that industrial structure matters for the well-being of the economy.[9] These views have led some governments to try to adopt industrial policies.[10] The result is nationally based innovation systems that treat technological innovation as a zero sum game. Governments have also used antidumping and investment policies to attract companies. But mature industrial countries should not use infant industry policies as such trade-distorting measures. If some governments use such policies, others will follow suit. Giving full national treatment to multinational corporations will blur the distinction between geographic location and national ownership and thus reduce the incentive to use such policies.

8. GATS prohibits limits on the number of service suppliers allowed, the value of transactions or assets, the total quantity of service output, employment, legal entities that can supply the service (for example, branches versus subsidiaries for banking), and participation of foreign capital. But these commitments apply only to services sectors listed by each country and only to the extent sector-specific limitations are not maintained. See Hoekman (1994).

9. Middle-income, fast-growing East Asian economies, such as Japan in the 1950s and 1960s and Korea and Taiwan in the 1970s and 1980s, believed that industrial success depended on the move from simple, light industries to heavy and chemical industries, and later to high-technology industries. Some U.S. advocates claim that government intervention is necessary to create high-paying jobs. Traditional market-oriented economists often dismiss this view: "Potato chips, computer chips, what's the difference?" The belief that industrial structure matters for wage levels and export performance is based on an argument that high-technology industries generate high value added and higher wages and spin off technological spillovers for other industries.

10. Ostry and Nelson (1995).

Nations currently differ in their willingness to grant national treatment. If the government monopolizes telecommunication services, for example, national treatment for a foreign telecommunications company means little. If domestic companies compete freely, national treatment means a great deal. GATT negotiations have shown that nations with relatively open and deregulated markets are reluctant to grant unconditional most-favored-nation treatment to countries in which market access is more limited. For similar reasons, reciprocity will be needed to achieve full national treatment.

National governments should be free to use subsidies and taxes, within internationally agreed-upon rules, to correct market failures as long as nations treat domestic and foreign companies equally. Governments operate within defined geographic boundaries. Companies know no such boundaries. Although language, culture, and history may give advantages to domestic companies, government policies must not. In particular, government-sponsored high-technology programs and government procurement should apply equally to all domestic companies, regardless of nationality of ownership. Ultimately, such participation should be extended to all companies headquartered within the club, regardless of their location. Private companies should be free to form alliances and joint ventures and to finance projects, provided they do not contravene rules for competition policy. In the end, all these rules should apply to the services sector.

TRANSITIONAL ARRANGEMENTS. Government officials will doubtless continue to worry if national companies trail the success of foreign enterprises or face problems on the world market. Because some current policies aim to counter these risks, governments may be loath to apply them equally to companies from all countries who join the club. Such an agreement could be phased in. Step one would require reductions in subsidies to ventures with purely national participation. Step two could involve mutual agreements among a few nations to open consortia to foreign companies when government subsidies or government procurement are involved. Ultimately, members of the club might be required, as a condition for membership, to share their best technologies with the rest of the consortium. The rule, of course, would reduce the incentive for leading nations to join but would allow for nondiscriminatory treatment.

REGULATORY OPENNESS. Nations will continue to have regulated sectors. Ultimately reciprocity of access for foreign companies in regulated sectors does not require national regulatory uniformity. The right to enter restricted sectors should be allocated through auctions open to both domestic and foreign nationals. In the short run increased transparency is critical. Measures should also be taken to increase foreign participation in activities in which entry is provided on the basis of regulatory discretion.

CORPORATE GOVERNANCE. Corporate governance differs internationally in accordance with historic and social circumstances.[11] No consensus exists on which approach is best. Efforts to impose uniform corporate governance should be rejected.

The debate over the Japanese corporate groups known as *keiretsu* became particularly heated in the Structural Impediments Initiative negotiations between Japan and the United States. Keiretsu are groups of firms, some of whom are linked as suppliers and purchasers (vertical keiretsu) and others of whom are drawn from several industries (horizontal keiretsu). U.S. representatives argued that keiretsu are exclusionary. The Japanese replied that they are efficient. Competition should settle this debate. If, for example, U.S. auto companies found that vertical networks similar to those of their Japanese competitors conferred a competitive advantage, this development would support Japanese contentions. But if an opening up of the Japanese distribution system eroded keiretsu ties, this development would support the U.S. claim that keiretsu are primarily instruments of exclusion. In general, as long as markets are competitive and contestable, companies should be free to set up supplier-distributor networks as they please.

Mechanisms for monitoring the performance of management differ among nations. Banks are large active shareholders in Germany and part of corporate groups in Japan. Pension funds are beginning to take more active roles in the United States, but other

11. Fukao (1995).

large institutional investors are passive and commercial banks do not hold equity. Competition, not regulation, should determine which approach works best in which countries. For example, French companies today may choose whether to incorporate using traditional French charters or German-style charters. Mutual recognition of alternative corporate forms should be extended. As long as markets are open, companies should enjoy wide discretion in choice of different corporate forms.

Standards

In all countries, national authorities and private organizations test products and set standards to ensure that consumers can use products from different producers and that products meet minimum standards of quality and performance. Unfortunately, both tests and standards can be and are used to obstruct international trade.

Problems arise because of conflicting goals. Uniform standards reduce production costs, intensify competition, and increase network benefits and product variety by lowering entry barriers. But uniformity can also restrict entry, reduce variety, and inhibit innovation. Accordingly, decisions on whether to impose uniformity or permit diversity should be made case by case. Some advocates of government-established standards claim that without them competition will erode standards. In fact, companies often take steps to ensure both compatibility and quality. Producers of high-quality products also have an interest in providing consumers with credible information on quality. In Japan, for example, obtaining a safe goods designation or a Japanese agricultural standards certification may be crucial for consumer acceptance. Such private bodies as the International Organization for Standardization and the International Electrotechnical Commission produce global compatibility standards.

In general, existing international institutions deal effectively with compatibility issues, although problems remain. Different national systems of weights and measures obstruct some trade. New proprietary technologies have posed problems—Betamax versus VHS for videocassette recorders, for example. Alan Sykes suggests that nations acting independently can conform standards for old technologies. Setting standards for new products, by contrast, is often difficult because of uncertainty about which technology is superior and because these uncertainties are the basis of a competitive struggle in which national interests differ. Although some differences can be resolved through negotiations and joint ventures, Sykes argues that the best policy may be to let countries compete and the market determine the best outcome.[12]

The Uruguay Round has made considerable progress on rules for establishing quality and performance standards. In fact, it has come close to establishing a club. GATT establishes a variety of principles: it requires use of the least restrictive means to achieve goals, it obliges countries that fail to use existing international standards to justify their behavior, it extends the domain of mutual recognition and the need to justify a failure to do so, and it extends the range of harmonized standards.

Scope remains, however, for improving cooperation in setting quality standards and in testing conformity with standards. Mutual acceptance of conformity should be required so that exporters can win certification. Currently, the need to pass tests in many countries involves waste and duplication and creates opportunities for protectionist abuse. Wherever possible, procedures for determining that products meet standards should themselves be standardized.

GATT relies on national governments to enforce these agreements. In addition, an international institution should collect information and report on regulatory practices of different club members. Just as GATT has recently begun to review trade policies, the club of standards should independently review standards and methods of setting them. It should identify technical barriers that obstruct trade and provide technical assistance on standards policies to member countries.

Technology

In general, free markets produce less research and development than is socially optimal because knowledge typically can be used

---

12. Sykes (1995).

by many people other than the person or business that pays for it. Accordingly, government intervention through patents or research subsidies can improve welfare by increasing the private profit from expenditures on research and development. For the same reason that companies invest less in research than is nationally optimal, countries may invest less than is globally optimal because benefits of greater knowledge increasingly spill across national borders. The U.S. experience since World War II is that technology cannot be contained inside national borders and that technological leadership is generally transitory. The proliferation of multinational corporations accelerates diffusion. Each nation has an interest in seeing that others spend more on research than they would choose to spend out of self-interest.

Accordingly, the proper forum for decisions on how much to spend on research and development has become international. For that reason, a science and technology foundation to which all member nations contribute would enhance global economic welfare. This club would focus on basic research that spills over among member nations and beyond and on scientific and pre-competitive generic technological research. It would leave product research to companies and nations. Basic research on medical products and on materials and support of basic mathematics, biology, and chemistry, and on how national economies interact are obvious candidates. In addition, such a club should foster the diffusion of technology to the least developed nations.

Natural Resources and Environment

International cooperation is clearly necessary when significant international environmental externalities occur.[13] The best option, where feasible, is voluntary negotiation. The convention on International Trade in Endangered Species and the Montreal Protocol on Substances that Deplete the Ozone Layer illustrate this approach. Reaching agreement may be difficult or even impossible when nations have different goals or attitudes toward risk or when they disagree on how to interpret scientific evidence. International

13. This section draws on Cooper (1994).

governance is required for dealing with access to the open oceans, the deep seabed, outer space, Antarctica, and anywhere there is an obvious need to avoid the overexploitation of resources that belong to no single nation.

When trade sanctions are necessary to force compliance, a club for the global environment should coordinate with the World Trade Organization to obtain explicit waivers from GATT rules. The club should provide technical and financial assistance to developing countries to meet such goals.

Environmental regulations that produce their effects primarily through international markets raise extremely divisive issues. The term *ecodumping* pejoratively describes weak environmental standards that encourage increased exports or attract foreign investment. In general, nations should enjoy considerable scope in tailoring environmental rules because incomes, tastes for a clean environment, and environmental conditions differ.[14] Moreover, allowing people in one country to set standards for other countries is dangerous because foreigners do not have to pay for exercising their sensibilities.

However, people should be free to reject goods produced with methods that offend them. The proper course in such cases is for countries first to try to negotiate international norms that prohibit or limit the offending activity. An environmental standards club could organize such negotiations with the goal of using measures that will distort trade as little as possible, that are based on good science, are easy to understand, operate through markets, and apply the polluter-pays principle. Countries could then use labels of origin so that buyers could boycott products from noncomplying countries. Countries at low development levels should be given time to adopt global minimum environmental standards, with the pace of compliance geared to the stage of development. However, this principle should not apply automatically even to developing countries when major threats, such as global warming or destruction of rain forest, are involved.

14. Cooper (1994)

Tax Policy

Taxing authority is one of the most jealously guarded aspects of national sovereignty.[15] This need not be a problem. In particular, where national tax systems affect each other only through markets, diversity in tax systems as in other functional areas of public policy should be encouraged. But where taxes cause market failure, other steps are necessary. Difficult situations include the use of taxes to affect terms of trade or where they promote evasion through smuggling. Furthermore, factor mobility limits the capacity of countries to use taxes to redistribute incomes.[16] Indeed, the viability of a differentiated tax system requires immobility of the taxed object. Payroll taxes can differ because most workers are relatively immobile. Similarly, taxes on natural resources can differ if resource endowments are internationally unequal. In contrast, sustaining different capital income tax rules is difficult because multinational companies can easily shift where they report income if it is taxed at its source or relocate their headquarters if it is taxed according to corporate residence. If capital can and does move freely to achieve the highest possible after-tax return, labor and owners of land will bear the full burden of capital taxes that differ from a worldwide average.

To preserve capital income taxation in an integrated world economy, nations have choices: to tax the worldwide income of national residents or to harmonize global taxation of capital. Some countries tax their residents' worldwide income, after giving credit for taxes paid to foreign tax authorities. But this practice creates serious problems. One is that the tax credit invites competition among national tax authorities over revenue from multinational corporations. Taxes paid by Japanese corporations to U.S. authorities, for example, are credited, with some limitations, against Japanese tax liability. Similar provisions are applied to U.S. multinationals by the U.S. Internal Revenue Service. The potential for competition among tax authorities increases, however, when governments claim the right, as some states have done in the United

15. This section draws on Tanzi (1995).
16. Tanzi (1995).

States, to base taxes on the global operations of companies with foreign affiliates under their jurisdiction.[17]

The second difficulty is that taxing capital without intergovernmental collaboration is becoming increasingly difficult. Assessing income within national boundaries is difficult enough. Assessing global income is an operational nightmare. Many nations prefer to tax at the source to capture revenues from multinational subsidiaries and nonresidents.

A possible solution is to form an international organization or club to harmonize policies on corporate taxation or at least impose minimal rules. Such collaboration will seem fanciful to many, and it will not occur soon. U.S. states do not, even now, collaborate in tax collection. But as mobility of production increases and sources of capital proliferate around the world, pressures for collaboration will intensify. Nations may remain as jealous over tax sovereignty as they are today, but they will face irresistible pressures to surrender some sovereignty to maintain revenues.

Macroeconomic Coordination

As nations integrate, macroeconomic policies in one country will increasingly affect business conditions in others.[18] If a country is small (in the sense that the country's policy decisions hardly have impacts on the rest of the world), the effect is essentially one-way. Large countries' decisions (for example, the U.S. interest hikes) affect small countries, but not vice versa. In fact, the adjustments in small countries are sometimes automatic: if the exchange rate is fixed to the large country's and no capital controls are imposed, then domestic monetary policy in the small country must mirror that in the large country.

Given the impact of policies among large countries, one natural response is to call for coordinated monetary and exchange rate policy to take account of the interactions that such interdepend-

---

17. This method, called the unitary tax, imposes tax on the proportion of global operations carried out within the borders of the taxing jurisdiction. The factors used in defining operations include sales, assets, and profits.

18. This section draws on Bryant (1995).

ence creates. For example, timing of interest cuts can be coordinated so that the effect on the exchange rate can be maximized (when changes are in opposite directions) or minimized (when changes are in the same direction). Similarly, fiscal policies could be adjusted.[19] But this is more easily said than done.

Although benefits of coordination among large economies may be present in theory, therefore, there are problems in practice. First of all, the countries may have conflicting views of what policies should be. As noted above, the 1980s have been marked both by periods in which agreement on policies was not possible (the first half of the decade) and by periods when it was (the second half). A second issue is that benefits from active coordination may be small in practice, and the costs of implementation in the form of constraining policies may outweigh the benefits.

Although genuinely joint execution of macroeconomic policy-making remains an unlikely prospect for the short term, therefore, considerable room remains for joint consultation. The G-7 summits and regular meetings at the OECD, the Bank of International Settlements, and the IMF have made some progress in coordinating macroeconomic and financial policies. Similarly, the Fund plays an essential role in providing macroeconomic policy surveillance and advice. Additional improvements need to be made in predicting the effects of policies and ensuring national compliance with agreements before nations can cede powers to a formal organization that would monitor policy and enforce coordination of national macroeconomic policies. As an interim measure, however, a macroeconomic club should start by carrying out exercises in macroeconomic modeling.

Exchange Rate Policy

In the course of the twentieth century, international exchange rates have been, at various times, fixed in relation to the value of gold or other currencies, fixed under the surveillance of the International Monetary Fund, and more or less flexible.[20] Even in the

---

19. See Bryant (1995) for a detailed discussion of macroeconomic policy coordination.
20. This section draws on Eichengreen (1994).

1990s the system is a mixed one. Many smaller countries adopt fixed exchange rates, while the exchange rates among the largest three economies—the United States, Japan, and Germany—remain floating. Similarly over time, the European experience has been mixed. The exchange rate mechanism under which the European currencies were tied to one another within narrow bands was once touted as a success in achieving converging inflation rates among its members and bringing down the exchange rate volatility. However, the turmoil in 1992 and 1993 took the British pound and Italian lira out of the mechanism and the band had to be widened. It remains to be seen whether member countries can proceed to a goal of single currency.

This mixed experience is not surprising given the considerations that go into determining an ideal exchange rate mechanism. As goods and financial markets become integrated, exchange rate volatility can become extremely disruptive. If factors of production are mobile, currency fluctuations can cause sizable reallocation of resources. Reallocation is costly in itself and may reflect incorrect judgments of long-term comparative advantage. For these reasons the efficiency benefits from use of a single currency can be large. However, use of a single currency or (its near equivalent) permanently fixed exchange rates also carries large costs. Because of capital mobility, a single currency would force nations to give up monetary policy as a stabilization instrument, a step that is feasible and desirable only (a) if cooperating nations can find a way to determine monetary policy that is responsive to the needs of each of the members; (b) if they experience similar economic disturbances and wish to respond to them similarly; (c) if labor is sufficiently mobile so that unemployment is evened out among them; and (d) if they are prepared to provide fiscal transfers where needed. Furthermore, the possibility of achieving a transition to a single currency when capital is highly mobile is in doubt because speculators will continuously challenge the credibility of exchange rate commitments. To succeed, therefore, the transition to a single currency must be fast.

These conditions make clear why a common global currency is unlikely to be adopted for the foreseeable future. At the regional level, however, and among countries whose conditions meet those enumerated above, common currencies may be more appropriate. As noted by Barry Eichengreen, skepticism is warranted about the feasibility of sustaining intermediate systems such as those based on target zones or on fixed bands or of a Bretton Woods-type system in the face of highly mobile capital without also taking measures to ensure compatible macroeconomic policies.

Existing Clubs

Some current international organizations could evolve into the clubs we envisage. In international labor standards and financial regulation, for instance, past negotiations have resulted in moderate coordination.

Labor Standards

Governments in most OECD countries are extensively involved in the labor market. They regulate work hours and the cost of overtime; mandate vacations, holidays, and sick leave; set minimum wages; restrict child and forced labor; prohibit discrimination; provide cash assistance to the unemployed, disabled, and retired; and set conditions for hiring and firing, unionization, and collective bargaining. Nations have generally taken these actions independently. The International Labor Organization has put forward voluntary standards, and GATT prohibits trade in goods made with forced labor. Additional efforts to bring these matters to international attention have been made in the United States and the European Union.

Most labor standards will be confined to local effects or will affect international trade and investment through market channels if labor mobility is slight. Despite the widespread perception that labor policies change trade and investment flows, the effects of government intervention in the labor market frequently are entirely local. Payroll taxes usually finance sick leave, maternity leave, and family leave. Many people think that such taxes raise employment costs and thereby affect resource allocation. But employers can usually adjust other elements of the package to keep their total costs from rising very much. In general, the supply of labor is fairly inelastic, and most payroll taxes result in lower wages rather than higher compensation over the long run.[21] Many labor standards reflect decisions that would have been taken in the marketplace anyway. In other cases, both compliance with binding measures and enforcement are weak and thus have no effects at all.

A few observers allege that tough international labor standards have positive economic effects, but the existence or importance of these effects is unproven and in any case, it is not clear why international pressure should be applied to force a government to take actions that are in its own interest. Furthermore, if labor standards reflect legitimate national preferences, it is unclear why other nations should be entitled to impose different standards.

In short, the case for allowing individual nations to set their own labor standards is strong, particularly when each nation bears the costs and benefits of its own standards. Even where standards affect other nations through market forces, diversity of social preferences means that diverse standards improve global welfare.

National actions that violate what others consider to be fundamental human rights—especially with regard to child labor—are more difficult to deal with. Where poverty explains the violations, rich nations should compensate poor nations for having to meet standards higher than the poor nations would choose. Or importing nations can label goods so that consumers are aware of how and where they were produced. The denial of trading opportunities should come only as a last resort and only for the most egregious violations.

Where nations agree on labor standards, as most do with respect to minimum standards, the credibility of domestic policies should be reinforced through international agreement. A labor club might expand the ILO's definitions of minimum labor standards and enforce them, for example, by extending the NAFTA principle under which nations define standards but compliance is subject to international supervision.

21. OECD (1993).

Beyond these minimum standards, club members should be allowed considerable autonomy. Moreover, such standards should take account of different levels of economic development. If labor market policies do not affect total labor costs or migration, there will be economic pressures for convergence of standards. If standards reflect national preferences, they will not be changed, even if they do have allocative consequences, as the noteworthy differences in minimum wages, occupational standards, and other labor standards across the fifty states of the United States attest.[22]

Financial Market Regulation

The internationalization of financial institutions presents important problems.[23] The first is risk. Because banking and financial institutions are closely linked, default in one bank can cause panic and failures throughout the systems. A related issue is how to establish fair competition among international financial institutions. National regulations differ in the scope of activities in which banks are allowed to engage. German-style, universal banking systems differ from the tightly constrained U.S. and Japanese systems. Enforcement mechanisms also differ among nations.

International measures are needed to ensure that financial markets are safe. One way is to establish international supervisory institutions. A second is to operate international "narrow banks," which provide limited services and are required to hold highly liquid and safe assets. A third way is to establish international standards that improve bank safety and provide clear responsibilities for central banks to honor international commitments of failed banks under their jurisdiction. An international standard, such as the Basel accord on bank capital, does not go far enough. International standards on risk evaluation may turn out to be more productive. Again, harmonization or worldwide uniform regulations are neither desirable nor feasible. How to deal with insolvent financial institutions and whether to keep banks and securities firms separate, for example, can be left to national regulations.

22. Ehrenberg (1994).
23. See Herring and Litan (1995).

What is needed in an internationally integrated financial market is a clear policy from central banks to prevent local crises from becoming international calamities. Central banks should publicly declare how they will deal with failures of large banks.[24] Punishing stockholders and related companies may be necessary. Depositors, domestic and international, should be protected. A rule on how to apportion a loss by international claim holders should be established now.

Increased cooperation among national regulatory authorities is essential. A financial regulation organization should be charged with improving this cooperation, setting standards, and allowing for single passports that allow financial firms headquartered in one club member to establish subsidiaries freely in other member countries. There should be a progression from national treatment based on equivalent and reciprocal access to mutual recognition and a single passport.

Regional Clubs: The Quest for Open Regionalism

Regional agreements have emerged as a prominent force in international economic governance in the past decade. The most extensive have been the successful implementation of the Europe 1992 program and the arrangements between the European Union and neighboring countries to form the European Economic Area and extend association arrangements to eastern European nations. The United States has signed agreements with Israel, Canada, and Mexico and initiated the Asia-Pacific Economic Cooperation forum. Australia and New Zealand have established free trade, as have the members of the Association of Southeast Asian Nations. Four South American countries—Argentina, Brazil, Paraguay, and Uruguay—have set up a customs union (Mercosur).

Some observers see in these agreements a sign that the world economy is breaking up into blocs as it did during the 1930s. Others see a repetition of the developing countries' failed efforts at establishing free trade areas in the 1950s and 1960s. However, the

24. Herring and Litan (1995).

motives behind the earlier regional initiatives were protectionist, while governments with market-oriented philosophies are implementing current policies. They are pursuing domestic liberalization and making an effort to attract foreign capital.

The new regionalism has gone well beyond simply removing border barriers.[25] The European Union has created a single market with a common policy on competition, mutual recognition of standards, and extensive policy harmonization. The North American Free Trade Agreement contains provisions dealing with investment and services and side agreements on labor standards and environmental protection. Australia and New Zealand have replaced their antidumping provisions with an agreement on competition policy.

Because regional arrangements both create and divert trade, free traders look upon them with ambivalence. Regional agreements stimulate trade by removing domestic barriers. But they also give insiders an advantage over outsiders, causing some diversion of purchases to less efficient sources.

The effects of regional arrangements that embody deeper integration could differ from those predicted by conventional trade theory. If deeper integration strengthens market forces, it may ease market entry for outsiders and create rather than divert external trade. Uniform European product standards or a single currency, for example, would facilitate entry into the market for all companies, not just ones located in Europe. Protectionist regulatory systems, however, even if deeply integrated, or managed trade, such as a common agricultural policy or the programs for protecting the steel industry of the European Union, could actually divert more trade than a shallow free trade area would. What matters is the precise nature of the new arrangements. For outsiders the question is whether the arrangements free up or constrain market pressures and whether they are transparent and open.

Regional alliances have important advantages over functional clubs for achieving deeper integration. They permit members to give concessions in one functional issue area for advantages they

25. Lawrence (1996).

receive in others, and they provide for economies in governance and oversight. Commitments to regional blocs may be more credible than commitments to large multilateral agreements, and governance may be easier to arrange. As the European Union and the North American Free Trade Agreement (NAFTA) demonstrate, countries may cede sovereignty more willingly to a neighbor than to a country half a world away because neighbors are more likely to have similar preferences. Furthermore, spillovers are more often regional than global, particularly with respect to migration, environmental damage, and tax evasion through smuggling. Finally, neighbors are often natural trading partners, so that integration causes relatively little trade diversion.

Regional arrangements also have limitations and dangers. A small group of nations may be unwilling to undertake deep institutional reforms that would automatically help outsiders. Canada and the United States, for example, would not remove agriculture subsidies bilaterally without similar concessions from competitors. Members of a regional club will always be tempted to resolve internal disputes at the expense of outsiders not represented in the negotiations. Finally, deep integration restricts the scope for autonomous policies, a matter of particular importance for developing countries.[26] Agreements among developed nations inevitably require reciprocal commitments. Preferential arrangements between developed and developing countries have typically provided for differential access. For example, the European Union provides preferential duty-free access to Caribbean and African nations under the Lomé Convention that the developing nations do not reciprocate. Countries that join regional clubs trade access to foreign markets in return for reductions in national economic sovereignty. Some analysts and officials in developing countries doubt whether this trade is worth making. They argue, for example, that Mexican products are unlikely to escape harassment from U.S. fair trade rules, while American companies will dominate the Mexican economy.

For countries with the capacity to attract foreign investment and that wish to undertake domestic institutional reform, this trade-off

---

26. Krueger (1995); Haggard (1995).

is nonetheless especially attractive. In conjunction with the North American Free Trade Agreement, for example, Mexico has adopted more rigorous intellectual property rules, improved its system for enforcing environmental standards and worker rights, eliminated several industrial policies, and improved the functioning of its democratic institutions. The Mexican government clearly believed these measures, some of which it might have taken anyway, were worthwhile to secure the benefits from NAFTA.

Other developing countries may, however, appropriately make different choices. The conditions required for joining deeper regional arrangements could preclude the special treatment that some developing countries require. The European Union agreed to compensate poorer countries for adopting stringent occupational and environmental standards. Other than loans to Mexico to assist in border environmental cleanups, NAFTA provided no such assistance. Poor nations denied such aid might decide that their best course would be to protect infant industries and use subsidies and other forms of industrial policy that are precluded by deep integration.

Rules for Regional Clubs

GATT has permitted regional arrangements that violate its most-favored-nation provisions, provided that the regional agreements do not raise external trade barriers and that they dismantle almost all internal barriers. GATT conditions place politically and operationally realistic discipline on regional agreements. We believe that proposals to compensate outsiders for trade diversion that does not involve higher external barriers are impractical, whatever their theoretical appeal. Although it may not fully insulate outsiders from trade diversion, article 24 of GATT, which authorizes preferential trading agreements, should be retained.

The most serious risk of trade diversion from regional trade agreements results not from the erection of new barriers, but from rules of origin, the application of antidumping rules, and perhaps misuse of product standards. It is better to curb such abuses by reforms in GATT rules of origin, dumping, and product standards than by changing article 24 rules governing preferential trading arrangements.

Regional clubs to achieve deeper integration in some functional areas should be encouraged, as long as they assist market forces. Deeply integrated regional clubs, as well as nations, can serve as the building units for international integration. But regional clubs should complement rather than replace multilateral organizations. Regional as well as global functional organizations should continue to adhere to GATT rules governing external trade and investment.

GATT does not require that preferential trading agreements be open to outsiders. However, regional arrangements that are conditionally open to all nations should be encouraged. For example, the report of the Asia-Pacific Economic Cooperation Eminent Persons Group has recommended that any country prepared to grant free trade to APEC members be allowed to join.[27] When members of a regional organization must surrender considerable sovereignty, as in the European Union, they should have the right to decide whether new members can join, even if applicants comply with conditions for membership. This power is important because members may legitimately fear that, as membership increases, they will lose influence over club decisions.

Nonetheless, the history of regional arrangements indicates that they tend to expand. The formation of the European Economic Community attracted the United Kingdom, Ireland, Denmark, and later Greece, Spain, and Portugal. As the European Community tightened economic and political bonds by adopting the Europe 1992 program, several countries of the European Free Trade Agreement initially sought closer and deeper arrangements under the Lisbon Agreements and later requested full membership. Similar pressures are operating for the eastern European countries and on Malta, Cyprus, and Turkey.

The North American Free Trade Agreement has unleashed similar expansionary processes. Mexico sought to counterbalance growing dependence on its more powerful NAFTA partners with

27. Eminent Persons Group (1994).

new initiatives toward the Pacific nations, Central and South America, and the OECD. The United States could not confine its attention to Mexico. President Bush invited other western hemisphere nations to sign individual free trade agreements with the United States or to come together in his Enterprise for the Americas initiative. President Clinton has expressed willingness to extend NAFTA to Chile and other nations in the western hemisphere. This U.S. invitation has stimulated increased interest in such regional Latin American initiatives as the Andean Pact and Mercosur. The United States has also felt pressures to pursue the APEC initiative with the Pacific nations.

The essential feature of the emerging regional arrangements is their diversity. Variety strengthens the case for clubs that can respond to the diverse needs of nations in different regions.

Existing and Emerging Regional Clubs

The three major economic regions of the world—Europe, America, and the Pacific—are following different paths to integration. The differences reflect diverse histories and varied current conditions. It is possible, but by no means certain or even likely, that their paths will converge in the foreseeable future.

EUROPE. Europe aims at a political union that includes a single market for goods and services and for capital and labor. The European Union is a clear example of a regional "club of clubs" that includes arrangements on competition, investment, financial institutions, labor and social standards, environmental protection, and macroeconomic coordination. Its Council of Ministers deals with all these topics. The European Union collects taxes, redistributes income, and administers common agricultural policy. It has greatly increased labor mobility and established a transnational governance system that can override the national sovereignty of member states on many matters.

The European internal market has improved access to outsiders in several respects. It replaces twelve diverse and often arcane decisionmaking processes with one multinational process that companies can follow from their headquarters or from a single office in Brussels. To be sure, a single standard can be crafted to inhibit market entry of outside companies, but all who wish to sell in Europe will find it easier to understand and comply with a single standard than with twelve. If the European Union successfully discourages efforts by each typically medium-sized European country to make sure that it has a full complement of industries, all market competitors will benefit. The line of reasoning, that deep integration actually increases the access of outsiders, implies that the rest of the world should support extension of EU membership to members of the European Free Trade Agreement and the countries of eastern Europe.

NAFTA AND BEYOND. The driving force behind the European Union is the desire for closer political relations. By contrast, the motives behind the North American Free Trade Agreement are largely economic. Indeed, Canada and Mexico are wary of U.S. political domination. The European Union and the North American Free Trade Agreement both achieve free trade and investment and call for national treatment, but integration is far deeper in the European Union than in NAFTA. NAFTA is a set of rules; it has no supporting institutional apparatus, other than panels to be drawn from member countries to settle disputes, and contains no provisions for coordinating the external trade policies of its members. The European Union features extensive governance and a common external trade policy.

Although less ambitious than the European Union, NAFTA will eventually remove almost all border barriers among two developed countries and one developing country. Besides achieving freer trade and investment, NAFTA and the side agreements that accompany it do constrain the national sovereignty of members in some ways. The agreement allows member countries to appeal national decisions on dumping and subsidies to an international dispute settlement panel. The side agreements are designed to ensure compliance with national labor and environmental standards rather than with minimum standards to which the members have subscribed. Multinational appeals mechanisms allow foreigners to help adjudicate disputes, thereby improving the transparency and impartiality of the process. These agreements will require major changes in Mexican legal practices.

The North American Free Trade Agreement shows developing countries that a regional club can help a developed economy improve its access to the U.S. market and thus strengthen internal reform and external liberalization. The agreement shows the United States that by offering greater access to its markets it can secure institutional changes abroad sought by U.S. companies, labor, and environmentalists.

In December 1994, in Miami, a hemispheric summit was held at which thirty-four leaders from throughout the Americas committed themselves to extend NAFTA and create a Free Trade Agreement of the Americas (FTAA) starting in 2005. President Clinton announced that the United States, together with its NAFTA partners Mexico and Canada, would initiate negotiations with Chile on accession to NAFTA.

In November 1994, in Bogor, Indonesia, the eighteen nations of APEC committed themselves to achieve free trade and investment in the region by 2020. Industrialized countries would proceed more rapidly and achieve such measures by 2010. But the precise content of this commitment remains to be determined in future negotiations.

Despite their proclamations in Indonesia, numerous nations in APEC remain skeptical that a formal traditional free trade agreement in the Pacific is an attractive option. Participating in such an agreement would of course be easy for economies such as Singapore and Hong Kong, which currently have almost no trade barriers. But for developing nations such as Indonesia, Thailand, China, and Korea, the required adjustments are considerable. APEC is unlikely in the foreseeable future to become a full-scale regional club like the European Union.

ASIAN PERSPECTIVES. Several Asian countries have watched developments of Europe 1992 and the North American Free Trade Agreement with great suspicion. Asian regional groupings of countries are typically much looser and less formal than the European Union or the North American Free Trade Agreement, and several have been largely symbolic or defensive.

Two factors explain the Asian approach to trade policy. First, many Asian nations credit the GATT system for their economic success. They have enjoyed spectacular growth in recent decades by exporting their products to the United States and the European Community. This export-oriented growth strategy has brought prosperity to Japan, Korea, Taiwan, Hong Kong, and Singapore. Now Malaysia, Thailand, Indonesia, China, and Vietnam have joined the economic chase. Many Asians wonder why they should tamper with a system that is working so well. Furthermore, they are deeply suspicious of the motives behind Europe 1992 and the North American Free Trade Agreement. They understand that the European Union represents political insurance for a single Europe. They also recognize that NAFTA will help cement Mexican democracy and make its liberalization permanent. Nonetheless, they fear that regional arrangements in Europe and North America could turn against them. Asian policymakers also worry that large NAFTA and EU markets could gang up on them and force trade concessions. Purely as a defensive measure, some Asian countries are now contemplating a regional grouping of their own.

Economic factors also militate against the formation of a free trade area in Asia. The region as a whole remains heavily dependent on its outside trade, but many Asian countries compete with each other. Formal trade barriers in Japan (with the exception of agriculture), Hong Kong, and Singapore are extremely low. And empirical studies suggest that the Pacific is a more natural free trade area than is the Asian region. In sum, therefore, an Asian free trade area would emerge only in response to global fragmentation or beleaguered isolation.

A second factor behind Asian economic policy is the enormous political diversity of the region. One of the most totalitarian regimes in the world (North Korea) stands between China and South Korea. China still maintains socialism. And resentment and fear of Japanese imperialism still remain in many Asian countries. While the cold war occupied Europe and North America, Asia experienced hot wars in Korea and in Vietnam. The United States maintains several bilateral military arrangements with Asian governments but no collective security agreement like NATO. As a result, Asian political integration trails that of Europe and North America.

Even without formal arrangements, intra-Asian trade and investment has expanded rapidly since the mid-1980s. Japan has surpassed the United States in exports to the region. Korean and Taiwanese investment in other Asian nations has soared. Rapid growth, not an increased bias toward intraregional transactions, explains this surge. Moreover, intraregional trade has not displaced external trade.

Booming exports and imports support growth not only in Asia but throughout the world. As long as barriers to exports and imports remain low, the development of economic bonds among Asian nations is desirable. From an economic point of view, an Asian economic region rivaling the European Union and the North American Free Trade Agreement should cause no concern.

THE FUTURE OF APEC. Views differ on the future role for APEC. It may never become as deeply integrated as the European Union, but it could help open the Asian economies to one other and the world. The Eminent Persons Group, senior advisers from the sixteen APEC economies, have suggested that the entire APEC region should start free trade in 2000 in all goods, services, and capital and complete the process by 2020 (by 2010 for developed countries in APEC).[28] Although the group urges individual APEC nations to liberalize unilaterally—so-called unconditional most-favored-nation treatment of nonmembers—it has not advocated this approach for all APEC economies, presumably because such a policy would weaken the incentives for nonmember countries to reduce their barriers to APEC exports and because the United States and several other countries are unlikely to agree to open markets to Asian exports without reciprocal treatment. Instead, the Eminent Persons Group proposes that APEC members agree to grant free entry to all APEC markets to any nonmember country that is willing to eliminate its trade barriers to APEC members. This step would encourage other nations to engage in similar liberalization, but the obstacles to its acceptance are formidable.

It is noteworthy, however, that GATT did not lay out an entire schedule to achieve world free trade. Members commit themselves

28. Eminent Persons Group (1994).

to free trade as a long-term goal, but they concentrate on taking small steps. Reducing barriers most in sectors where political resistance has been least has allowed trade negotiators to choose when to fight protectionist forces and has given them time to build supporting coalitions. By contrast, a proposal calling for complete liberalization in all sectors would provoke across-the-board resistance from every group with a protected market. Consider, for example, the reactions of Korean and Japanese farmers to such a proposal if they were abruptly forced to compete with low-cost agriculture in Thailand and the United States. Or imagine the panic U.S. textile producers would feel at the prospect of complete free trade with China.

Although APEC has an uncertain future as a free trade area, it holds promise if it seeks to implement measures for deeper integration of behind-the-border policies. This assertion seems paradoxical and counterintuitive, but it rests on the special characteristics of Asian economies. Many barriers to free trade and investment in APEC nations result from domestic regulatory, administrative, and private practices that restrict the entry of newcomers, not from barriers at the border. Tariffs can be removed, but foreigners may still find it difficult to sell or invest if regulations are obscure, if policymakers favor domestic companies, or if domestic companies collude to restrict entry. Many Americans believe, for example, that such internal policies and practices explain why Japanese imports of manufactured goods and foreign direct investment are so limited. The United States would not agree to eliminate border barriers unless progress was made on these issues. For these reasons, it may be easier and more significant in the Pacific to achieve deep integration than it would be to create a traditional free trade area.

The primary goal of APEC should be to make markets more contestable. If regional arrangements deal first with domestic practices that mute market forces, they will make entry for outsiders easier and create rather than divert external trade. Interest in deregulation is growing in Japan, Korea, and other Asian nations. APEC should also consider ways to make regulations simpler and easier to understand, extend national treatment to foreign-owned companies, increase access for foreign companies to financial and other regulated sectors, cooperate in competition policies, and reduce domestic agricultural subsidies. Many countries might find it easier to pursue these measures through an international agreement than through bilateral negotiations. Agreements in these areas would provide benefits both within and beyond the APEC region. They would serve as a crucial complement to an ambitious program of cutting tariffs and quotas and represent an important contribution to the world economy even if the tariff-cutting program should flounder.

Many Asian countries doubt the need for such measures, because their growth is so strong. Eventually, however, the growth of potential output will slow. It would be easier to take steps to integrate in the currently favorable climate of strong growth than it would be after underlying growth has slowed.

In sum, regional clubs that advance deeper, market-oriented integration could be crucial in promoting worldwide economic integration. To do so, however, regional free trade associations must forgo rules of origin and antidumping provisions that divert trade from outsiders. The vital test of policies that go beyond removing border barriers is whether they make internal markets more contestable. Measures that do so will benefit both insiders and outsiders and should be supported. Measures that do not should be challenged.

The Global Community of Clubs

Besides functional and regional clubs, one or more multilateral institutions are needed. Without multilateral oversight, uncoordinated policies of countries or of functional or regional clubs would run the risk of fragmentation and inconsistency. A multilateral organization would coordinate the activities of regional and functional organizations; encourage dialogue and interaction among them, particularly on such crosscutting questions as environmental protection measures that affect trade; ensure that they adhere to basic norms; and help them deal with interclub disputes. This overarching organization would also initiate new clubs. The multilateral institution could grow out of the World Trade Organization or the International Monetary Fund, or it could be developed separately. We call this organization the club of clubs. Thus the system in which the club arrangements would be combined is more than just the sum of its parts. The club of clubs would be instrumental in achieving an open economic enviroment.

All countries accepting the basic procedural rules of such an oversight institution would be able to join all subsidiary clubs. Outsiders could challenge the rules of any specific club under procedures established by the club of clubs, as they now can question regional arrangements under GATT article 24. The club would ensure open markets by eliminating border barriers and by ensuring that agreements on deeper integration complement rather than supplant market forces. Low tariffs and the absence of border barriers remain necessary to ensure that markets are open. Deeper integration complements rather than supplants shallow integration.

Imperatives and Pitfalls

This three-tier structure raises several questions. First, why are regional arrangements desirable? Why not just make functional clubs? Our answer is that for the foreseeable future differences in circumstances and values make regionalism inescapable. Deep integration reveals profound national differences on such issues as workers' rights, disclosure rules, welfare policy, and income redistribution. These questions increasingly affect trade. Yet global agreement on how to deal with them may never be achievable and certainly lies in the distant future. Regional groupings of like-minded nations can discuss these politically sensitive issues without risking immediate deadlock. Obviously, regionalism risks global fragmentation into blocs that are internally open but closed to the external world. That risk highlights the importance of a global system—a community of clubs—in which an overarching club of clubs would provide a bridge among regional and functional organizations.

Why not have all nations participate in all clubs? The answer, like the answer to the first question, is that this objective is a desirable long-term goal, but not all nations are prepared to join all functional clubs. Accordingly, our structure represents an effort to accommodate national diversity. It is essential that in each regional and functional club, members accept common obligations. Although developing countries may be given more time to meet these obligations, their special treatment should not be permanent. Accordingly, given diverse national circumstances, this means either agreeing to extremely weak rules (the lowest common denominator) or making these rules stronger and membership more limited. We have chosen the latter and believe the overall membership structure of these clubs will have a variable geometry.

Why not let clubs function independently? Our answer is that linking issues permits trade-offs and side payments. And linking brings economies of scale and scope in governance. The organization can use one body to settle disputes and one staff instead of the many that separate organizations would require. But linking issues also entails risks. It can lead to overloaded agendas that hamper achievement of final settlements, as the recent Uruguay Round painfully illustrated.

Are rules necessary to ensure consistency among clubs? If so, what should they be? Regional and functional clubs may act inconsistently. Each functional club would have to determine the compatibility of regional club membership with its rules. However, these systems need not conflict. Regions as well as individual nations are potential members of functional clubs. For example, the European Union could participate as a single entity in GATT, or the European Monetary System could join with the United States and Japan in a target zone arrangement. Mutual recognition could also help avoid inconsistencies. No problem arises if regional organizations adopt tougher standards than those of a global functional club. If regional norms were weaker, regional members seeking to join the global club would have to adopt higher standards.

The interaction between the Bank for International Settlements and the European Union regarding banking supervision illustrates complex interaction between functional and regional clubs (box 4–1).

What will be the distribution of power within clubs? Will they be dominated by large and powerful members? Our answer is that the

Box 4-1. Interaction between Functional and
Regional Entities

The Cooke Committee of the Bank for International Settlements developed prudential ratios for bank capitalization. National banking authorities then transferred these standards into national regulations. The ratios had a major effect on national banking systems, such as that of the Japanese. They also were a cornerstone in the second banking directive that the European Community developed. That directive includes a provision, the single banking passport, based on the principle of mutual recognition, which has no equivalent at the Bank for International Settlements. Yet to benefit from the single banking passport, European Community members decided to harmonize core elements in their banking regulations, using the BIS ratios as central prudential instruments. In that case, decisions moved from the Bank for International Settlements, a kind of club of clubs, to the regional level. Given this change, however, it will become more difficult for the BIS to revise its approach.

approach proposed here avoids the power politics of imperial harmonization. The club of clubs and functional clubs would have broad membership. Inevitably, larger nations would have more influence than would smaller ones. But smaller participants could form coalitions to avoid dominance by larger members, and larger entities would tend to balance and counteract one another.

Furthermore, even major participants would have an interest in implementing rules to restrain other countries and deter opportunistic action by powerful domestic interest groups. Most clubs, and the club of clubs, should function from consensus, although larger donors would have disproportionate influence on policies that involve large resource transfers. And all clubs should have dispute settlement and enforcement mechanisms that accord small countries equal protection under club rules.

WTO Plus?

The new World Trade Organization might evolve into a supervisory club. For it to do so, however, two steps would be necessary. The first is to depart from the principle that all GATT members receive unconditional most-favored-nation treatment, a departure that has precedent, although it would reverse one of the achievements of the Uruguay Round. In the Tokyo Round, GATT members negotiated codes to which not all members subscribed. However, in the Uruguay Round the rules were universalized, and revised versions of the codes have been included in the basic articles that apply to all members.

The second modification necessary if the World Trade Organization is to function as a club of clubs would be to include in its charter the investment and other internal policies that form the agenda of deep integration. It would be essential to permit countries to integrate at different speeds. Some members could form clubs such as the one we have proposed to ensure internationally contestable markets that are more revolutionary than any of the trade measures so far debated. Only those countries interested in further liberalization and harmonization of their domestic economies would participate. Nonetheless, only some nations in the World Trade Organization would be likely to accept the restraints on national sovereignty that such an initiative would require.

Intermediate Measures

International cooperation begins with international consultation, common aspirations, and shared information. The most successful exercise in deeper international integration, the Europe 1992 program, began with a vision of a single European market for goods, services, capital, and labor. The European Commission then laid out the steps necessary to achieve the vision. A strong, credible commitment to it by participating nations shaped expectations of key corporate and government decisionmakers whose actions helped realize the vision. The adoption by many countries of a long-term commitment to the goal of an open and diverse international community could similarly help steer the expectations and affect the behavior of crucial decisionmakers. In contrast, a widespread fear that international cooperation is breaking down could produce inward-looking policies, global fragmentation, and managed trade. The sense that other nations have very different goals could similarly engender conflict. Beliefs can be self-fulfilling.

Shared knowledge can help realize the vision of an open world economy. Global organizations should promote research by major research organizations or think tanks that could be part of the club of clubs. Functional clubs could take over these tasks, although the think tanks could continue to offer independent critical analysis. Such institutions could identify the major issues on which international policy cooperation is needed, synthesize existing knowledge and encourage new research, systematically review domestic policies relevant to other countries, apprise and advise governments on policies to improve transparency and openness, and stimulate increased contacts between policymakers and others in critically important areas.

The Organization for Economic Cooperation and Development performs some of these functions already. It facilitates international comparisons and promotes communication among national policymakers. The OECD also already includes the fifteen members of the European Union, three members of the North American Free Trade Agreement, and a few Pacific countries. With expanded membership, it could become a prototypical global think tank. Other major international organizations could also contribute. The World Trade Organization has new trade policy review mechanisms. The International Monetary Fund and the World Bank both regularly review their members' policies and practices. These activities should be expanded. Better information can improve policy by enabling countries to set their own policies based on a knowledge of what other countries intend to do.[29]

Although calls to create new international organizations always seem visionary, the next few years hold great opportunities. In competition policy, a new organization we have called the International Competition Policy Office could begin modestly and with little controversy to collect and disseminate information. Initially, this organization would merely cooperate with local authorities; later it could recommend actions and intervene in actions that had

29. Bryant (1995).

serious implications for global markets. An International Science Foundation could be created soon and start modestly to subsidize basic and generic research. Initial funding could be modest and increase when and as member nations recognized the value of its activities.

Finally, to coordinate macroeconomic policy, the relevant agencies could begin by improving data collection and helping nations calibrate the models they use in setting monetary and fiscal policy. Governments could engage in joint exercises to test policy combinations in experimental rather than binding arrangements. Governments could then move on to experiments with voluntary policy coordination and, perhaps, eventually to binding arrangements if it became clear that the advantages of improved performance outweighed loss of policy autonomy.

Measures Outside the Club Framework

Besides official international collaboration, unilateral government actions, informal contact among officials, and, most importantly, contact among private companies and nongovernmental organizations could advance global economic integration.

The best international policy begins at home—the slogan "think globally, act locally" best captures what we mean.[30] International collaboration will work well only if individual economies independently prepare themselves to participate fully in a more deeply integrated global economy. Reforms of individual agricultural support systems are essential if global trade in agriculture is to be reformed. Domestic regulations must be clear and domestic markets must be open and contestable before foreigners can participate. The North American Free Trade Agreement was possible only because of the liberalization of the Mexican economy. Nations today are subject to increased competitive pressures. These forces will not necessarily cause identical practices, but they will help make them attractive locations for international production.

The typical national civil servant in Europe spends two days a week on European matters, often in Brussels or in another Euro-

---

30. Paarlberg (1995).

pean city.[31] The number of national civil servants involved in these European interactions is ten times greater than the Brussels bureaucracy and ten times greater than the number of political appointees in a new U.S. administration. Discussions among experts going to Basel every other week are an integration tool.

In the international harmonization of standards, the formation of international joint research programs, and the construction of global trading networks, private companies rather than governments have taken the lead to increase global integration. Governments should not stand in the way of these efforts, which are likely to reflect genuine market-driven needs. Moreover, governments should appreciate that to achieve true trust and mutual understanding, people-to-people contact rather than official agreement on rules and procedures is critical.

31. Wallace (1994).

Chapter 5

Summary

The world has made remarkable progress during the past five decades in lowering the barriers on goods and investment that were erected before World War II. Increased integration has contributed to an unprecedented period of growth and prosperity. But as border barriers have been lowered, differences in national domestic policies have been exposed to international scrutiny. These domestic policies are creating new tensions and conflicts.

Past, Future, and Vision

As the twentieth century comes to a close, three roads to the economic future lie before economic policymakers. They can rely on the historical policies of reducing at-the-border trade barriers, the agenda of shallow integration. They can seek to harmonize and reconcile national differences, the agenda of deeper integration. Or they can reverse previous liberalization and reassert national autonomy. Which road today's leaders choose will shape the world in which their children and grandchildren live.

Scenarios

These approaches suggest three scenarios. In the world of the *invisible hand* nation-states would maintain open borders for trade and capital but engage in little international coordination. Competition in trade and international capital markets would produce automatic pressures for harmonization. Under an alternative scenario, *global fragmentation,* nations would resurrect protective barriers. Finally, major economies such as the United States or the European Union may impose *imperial harmonization,* under which they would force smaller nations to adopt designated standards and regulations.

The most pessimistic of these scenarios is global fragmentation. To the extent that it is realized, forces of protectionism and nationalism would undermine the world's ability to maintain open economies and global cooperation, with costly consequences. Such fragmentation would threaten the prospects of both emerging and developed nations. Emerging nations would back away from the outwardly oriented policies necessary for sustained growth. Developed nations would sacrifice opportunities for economies of scale and growth through specialization.

Imperial harmonization is a less pessimistic vision, but it would increase global political disparities. It would permit only some nations to fully realize the gains from international cooperation and would suppress diversity. A world governed by the invisible hand is a more optimistic vision because it would permit national diversity and encourage harmonization through market pressures. Without international governance, however, opportunistic national behavior could be expected, some problems would prove insoluble, and the least fortunate nations would be totally neglected.

None of these scenarios is ideal. A more desirable outcome would avoid the dangers of global fragmentation by keeping nations open while achieving the diversity of the invisible hand and more equitable international governance than would be likely under imperial harmonization. In short, the desirable outcome would involve a world community of nations marked by openness, diversity, and cohesion.

Analytical Considerations

The world is organized into nation-states, and it is generally presumed that the nation is the appropriate jurisdictional level of governance. Under some circumstances, however, international governance may produce better results than would emerge from independent and uncoordinated national action.

The argument that shallow integration would produce internationally the best results depends on two assumptions: that markets operate efficiently—in other words that there are no international market failures—and that political systems are legitimate —that national governments reflect the interests of their citizens and thus no constraints need be imposed on their actions, an assumption analogous to consumer sovereignty. If markets or political systems fail, the case for international cooperation or discipline would strengthen.

The decision on when the case for international cooperation is strong enough for nations to cede some part of their autonomy or to force other nations to cede some autonomy is sensitive and subtle. International cooperation permits nations to internalize and deal with market failures, such as those arising when one nation's production generates pollution in another. It permits nations to cooperate to provide international public goods, such as basic scientific research, to police opportunistic national actions, and to take advantage of international economies of scale. But decentralized national decisionmaking accommodates diversity in national preferences and conditions, the need for accountable government, uncertainty about appropriate policies, the importance of common historical and cultural experiences in developing communal solidarity, and the ability to realize economies of scope in governance.

A Community of Nations

The insights from these possibilities and analytical considerations point to the desirability of a global community of nations that balances openness, diversity, and cohesion. Openness improves competition and discourages trade and industrial policies that exploit monopoly power. Diversity accommodates varying national conditions and preferences and allows for innovation and experimentation. Cohesion and trust in one another's institutions and practices and in international institutions is essential if increased openness is to be viable.

Taken to extremes, any one of these attributes could undermine the others. As an American, a European, and a Japanese, we believe that each of our societies offers essential ingredients for realizing this vision. From America, the most open of our societies, we take the lesson of transparency and an open system based on rules. From Europe, the most diverse, we take the principles of mutual recognition and subsidiarity. From Japan, the most cohesive of our countries, we take the principle of cooperation based on trust and consensus. Our vision combines these elements in a set of proposals.

These principles should be applied in international organizations and agreements that nations join voluntarily. These entities, which we call clubs for simplicity, take three forms. *Functional clubs* are devoted to single or related issues such as competition policy, standards policy, financial regulation, environmental protection, labor and human rights, and macroeconomic coordination. Examples of functional clubs now in existence are the Bank for International Settlements and the International Labor Organization. *Regional clubs* deal with several functional areas simultaneously. Examples of regional clubs include the European Union, the North American Free Trade Agreement, and Asia-Pacific Economic Cooperation. Finally, one or more *global coordinating clubs* should deal with linkages among issues. No such global organization now exists, but the United Nations, the World Trade Organization, and the Organization for Economic Cooperation and Development embody elements of such an entity. All clubs should be open to all nations prepared to abide by the obligations of membership. The only exception would be regional clubs that aim at moving toward nationhood.

To achieve transparency, clubs would institutionalize international information sharing, frequent exchanges among officials, and open and transparent systems for determining and enforcing rules. To ensure diversity, the powers of the clubs should be used only when strictly necessary. For example, members would retain the freedom to choose both the specific levels and means by which agreed norms and standards are to be achieved. In addition, countries would in general grant one another mutual recognition so long as all adhered to minimum standards. Finally, to bolster cohesion, members would enjoy equal treatment, with decision-making based on consensus unless there are exceptional circumstances. Such exceptions could include situations in which members make very unequal contributions to club resources or in which the least developed countries are given longer transitional periods to meet club obligations. Clubs would also place a strong emphasis on providing technical and financial assistance to developing countries seeking to upgrade their capacity to meet club norms and would make special efforts to provide resources to the least developed nations.

Functional Clubs

A few brief examples illustrate how functional clubs could evolve. In financial market regulation, for example, one goal should be to increase cooperation among national regulatory authorities. The aim should be to progress from providing national treatment based on equivalent and reciprocal access to mutual recognition and a single passport, which would allow firms from any nations in the club to operate in others.

A functional organization could evolve from the International Labor Organization to deal with labor standards. The ILO has broad-based membership and reflects concerns of both developed and developing countries. Individual nations should be given scope for differentiation in applying labor standards, particularly when the costs and benefits of such standards are fully borne by the nation itself. Even where these standards affect others through market forces, standards that reflect diverse social preferences will increase global welfare. Where nations share a consensus on labor standards—prohibition on trade in goods produced by coerced labor and certain other minimum standards, for example—international agreement should reinforce domestic policies. Behavior that impinges on ideas of fundamental human rights is more difficult to deal with. One solution is to induce poor nations to comply by offering them compensation. Alternatively, importers could use labeling or moral suasion to discourage exporters from engaging in repugnant practices. The denial of trading opportunities should come only as a last resort and only in the most egregious cases.

No effective international functional organizations exist in some areas. A new competition club could arise either as part of the World Trade Organization or as an independent institution. Members of this club would no longer apply the current trade rules to discourage dumping and subsidies. Instead, a new arrangement would ensure that international markets are open and contestable by applying competition policies. Club members would also agree to enforce a code of conduct for domestic regulation, guarantee foreign investors full nondiscriminatory treatment (in government procurement and participation in government-sponsored technology consortia), and provide for mutual recognition of differing forms of corporate governance.

A new global science and technology foundation could allocate funds for basic and precompetitive generic technological research on a competitive basis. This organization would give preference to programs that involve consortia made up of companies or participants from several member nations. Grants would be given for more basic research, whose fruits would be globally accessible, and for upgrading technology in the least developed nations.

A new club on product standards would implement mutual acceptance of conformity-testing results. Such an entity would build on the accomplishments of the Uruguay Round of multilateral trade negotiations. Where standards differ, exporters would be able to obtain certification in their home countries that their products meet particular foreign standards. The club would actively monitor standards and regulatory practices in club members, encourage exchanges and cooperation among national bodies, and issue reports and settle members' disputes. Finally, issues of international environmental protection have become sufficiently important to justify a club that focuses on many of these questions.

Functional clubs could be helpful in two other areas where progress on a broad global level is likely to be slow. These relate to the most fundamental attributes of national sovereignty—taxes and international finance. Many nations use taxes to redistribute incomes. Such policies are difficult to sustain when the object of taxation is internationally mobile. Indeed, the viability of an internationally differentiated tax system requires some degree of immobility in the object of taxation. The increasing ability of multinational companies to shift where they report income complicates the imposition of differentiated entity-level taxes. One partial solution is to tax people who receive income rather than companies that produce it. If entity-level taxes are to survive, it may be necessary to coordinate tax systems or to develop greatly expanded collaboration among taxing authorities.

Achieving coordination is even harder in managing macroeconomic policy. Some nations, especially in regional arrangements, will find it useful and feasible to adopt common currency areas. But the restraints on national sovereignty resulting from surrendering monetary autonomy to multilateral arrangements remain unacceptable to most nations, and the knowledge base is inadequate for detailed coordination arrangements. Nonetheless consultation can play a useful role, particularly in the face of common problems.

Regional Clubs

Deep regional integration could be better or worse for outsiders than traditional preferential trading arrangements. What counts is the nature of regional arrangements. Outsiders would gain if arrangements facilitate rather than retard market pressures. Thus regional clubs organized to achieve deeper integration in several functional areas should be encouraged, as long as they operate to increase the scope of market forces. Deeply integrated regional clubs could even serve as the building blocks for global integration.

The external trade and investment relations of all regional groups should continue to adhere to rules laid out in the General Agreement on Tariffs and Trade. Regional groups should also participate in any global functional clubs. As in the case of functional arrangements, regional clubs may be inappropriate for some developing nations.

The Community of Clubs

One or more multilateral institutions are necessary to coordinate functional and regional organizations, initiate new clubs, encourage dialogue and interaction among clubs (particularly on such cross-cutting issues as environmental protection measures that affect trade), ensure that functional clubs conform to basic norms and disciplines, and help deal with disputes among clubs.

Progress toward a global community also has other requirements: information, national unilateral measures to improve the openness of economies to outsiders, increased informal interaction by national officials, and increased cooperation between nongovernmental organizations and companies.

References

Albert, Michel. 1993. *Capitalism against Capitalism.* London: Whurr.

Baumol, William J., and Wallace E. Oates. 1975. *The Theory of Environmental Policy: Externalities, Public Outlays and the Quality of Life.* Prentice-Hall.

Bordo, Michael D., and Barry Eichengreen, eds. 1993. *A Retrospective on the Bretton Woods System: Lessons for International Monetary Reform.* Unversity of Chicago Press.

Bosworth, Barry, and Gur Ofer. 1995. *Reforming Planned Economies in an Integrating World Economy.* Brookings.

Brander, James A., and Barbara J. Spencer. 1985. "Export Subsidies and International Market Share Rivalry." *Journal of International Economics* 18 (February): 83–100.

Brenton, Tony. 1994. *The Greening of Machiavelli: The Evolution of International Environmental Politics.* London: Royal Institute of International Affairs.

Bryant, Ralph C. 1995. *International Coordination of National Stabilization Policies.* Brookings.

Buiter, Willem H., and Kenneth M. Kletzer. 1992. "Fiscal Policy Coordination as Fiscal Federalism: Economic Integration, Public Goods and Efficiency in Growing Economies." *European Economic Review* 36 (April): 647–53.

Centre for Economic Policy Research. 1993. *Making Sense of Subsidiarity: How Much Centralization for Europe?* London.

Collins, Susan M. Forthcoming. *Distributive Issues: A Constraint on Global Integration.* Brookings.

Cooper, Richard N. 1994. *Environment and Resource Policies for the World Economy.* Brookings.

Cornes, Richard, and Todd Sandler. 1986. *The Theory of Externalities, Public Goods and Club Goods.* Cambridge University Press.

Ehrenberg, Ronald G. 1994. *Labor Markets and Integrating National Economies.* Brookings.

Eichengreen, Barry. 1994. *International Monetary Arrangements for the 21st Century.* Brookings.

Eminent Persons Group. 1994. "Achieving the APEC Vision: Free and Open Trade in the Asia Pacific." Singapore: APEC Secretariat.

Fukao, Mitsuhiro. 1995. *Financial Integration, Corporate Governance, and the Performance of Multinational Companies*. Brookings.

Hampden-Turner, Charles, and Alfons Trompenaars. 1993. *The Seven Cultures of Capitalism: Value Systems for Creating Wealth in the United States, Japan, Germany, France, Britain, Sweden, and the Netherlands*. Currency/Doubleday.

Haggard, Stephan. 1995. *Developing Nations and the Politics of Global Integration*. Brookings.

Helpman, Elhanan, and Paul R. Krugman. 1985. *Market Structure and Foreign Trade: Increasing Returns, Imperfect Competition, and the International Economy*. MIT Press.

Herring, Richard J., and Robert E. Litan. 1995. *Financial Regulation in the Global Economy*. Brookings.

Hoekman, Bernard. 1994. "Services and Intellectual Property Rights." In *The New GATT: Implications for the United States*, edited by Susan M. Collins and Barry P. Bosworth, 84–121. Brookings.

Johnson, Harry G. 1987. "Optimal Trade Intervention in the Presence of Domestic Distortions." In *International Trade: Selected Readings*, edited by Jagdish N. Bhagwati, 235–63. MIT Press.

Krueger, Anne O. 1995. *Trade Policies and Developing Nations*. Brookings.

Lawrence, Robert Z. 1996. *Regionalism, Multilateralism and Deeper Integration*. Brookings.

Low, Patrick. 1993. *Trading Free: The GATT and U.S. Trade Policy*. New York: Twentieth Century Fund Press.

McKinnon, Ronald I. 1963. "Optimum Currency Areas." *American Economic Review* 53 (September): 717–25.

Meadows, Donella H. and others. 1972. *The Limits to Growth*. Universe Books.

Mundell, Robert A. 1961. "A Theory of Optimum Currency Areas." *American Economic Review* 51 (November): 657–65.

Ohmae, Kenichi. 1993. "The Rise of the Region State." *Foreign Affairs* 72 (Spring): 78–87.

Organization for Economic Cooperation and Development. 1993. *Employment Outlook*. Paris.

Ostry, Sylvia, and Richard R. Nelson. 1995. *Techno-Nationalism and Techno-Globalism: Conflict and Cooperation*. Brookings.

Paarlberg, Robert L. 1995. *Leadership Abroad Begins at Home: U.S. Foreign Economic Policy after the Cold War*. Brookings.

Perot, H. Ross, and Pat Choate. 1993. *Save Your Job, Save Our Country: Why NAFTA Must Be Stopped—Now*. Hyperion.

Porter, Michael E. 1990. *The Competitive Advantage of Nations*. Free Press.

Putnam, Robert D., and C. Randall Henning. 1989. "The Bonn Summit of 1978: A Case Study in Coordination." In *Can Nations Agree? Issues in International Economic Cooperation*, edited by Richard N. Cooper, 12–140. Brookings.

Rivlin, Alice M. 1992. *Reviving the American Dream: The Economy, the States and the Federal Government*. Brookings.

Rutland, Peter. Forthcoming. *Russia, Eurasia, and the Global Economy.* Brookings.

Scherer, F. M. 1994. *Competition Policies for an Integrated World Economy.* Brookings.

Shirk, Susan. 1994. *How China Opened Its Door: The Political Success of the PRC's Foreign Trade and Investment Reforms.* Brookings.

Stiglitz, Joseph. E. 1977. "The Theory of Local Public Goods." *In The Economics of Public Services,* edited by Martin S. Feldstein and Robert P. Inman, 274–332. Macmillan.

Sykes, Alan. 1995. *Product Standards for Internationally Integrated Goods Markets.* Brookings.

Tanzi, Vito. 1995. *Taxation in an Integrating World.* Brookings.

Thurow, Lester C. 1992. *Head to Head: The Coming Economic Battle among Japan, Europe, and America.* Morrow.

Tiebout, Charles M. 1956. "A Pure Theory of Local Expenditures." *Journal of Political Economy* 64 (October): 416–24.

Tinbergen, Jan. 1954. *International Economic Integration.* Amsterdam: Elsevier.

Wallace, William. 1994. *Regional Integration: The West European Experience.* Brookings.

World Commission on Environment and Development. 1987. *Our Common Future.* Oxford University Press.

Index

DATE DUE